P9-DEF-063

The Power Sermon

The Power Sermon

Countdown to Quality Messages for Maximum Impact

Reg Grant & John Reed

Baker Books
A Division of Baker Book House Co.
Grand Rapids, Michigan 49516

© 1993 by Reg Grant and John Reed

Published by Baker Books
A division of Baker Book House Company
P.O. Box 6287, Grand Rapids, Michigan 49516-6287

Printed in the United States of America

All rights reserved. No part of this publication may be reproduced, stored in a retrieval system, or transmitted in any form or by any means—electronic, mechanical, photocopy, recording, or any other—without the prior written permission of the publisher. The only exception is brief quotations in printed reviews.

Library of Congress Cataloging-in-Publication Data

Grant, Reg, 1954–
    The power sermon : countdown to quality messages for maximum
    impact / Reg Grant & John Reed.
        p.   cm.
    Includes bibliographical references.
    ISBN 0-8010-3852-9
    1. Preaching. I. Reed, John (John W.), 1927– . II. Title.
BV4211.2.G675 1993
251—dc20   92-37763

Unless otherwise noted, Scripture is taken from the HOLY BIBLE, NEW INTERNATIONAL VERSION®. Copyright © 1973, 1978, 1984 by International Bible Society. Used by permission of Zondervan Publishing House. All rights reserved. The "NIV" and "New International Version" trademarks are registered in the United States Patent and Trademark Office by International Bible Society. Use of either trademark requires the permission of International Bible Society.

Scripture marked NASB is from the New American Standard Bible, © the Lockman Foundation 1960, 1962, 1963, 1968, 1971, 1972, 1973, 1975, 1977.

This book is, and we are,
forever dedicated
to Lauren and Erris.

9

87830

Contents

Introduction

Countdown: T minus eleven questions to sermon liftoff and counting:

Eleven. What is this sermon about?
Ten. What does the rest of the Bible say about my subject?
Nine. Where is the sermon going?
Eight. How do I get started?
Seven. How do I keep from missing a turn?
Six. What do I do when I arrive at my destination?
Five. How do I keep the trip interesting and enjoyable?
Four. How can I make sure the style is right for the trip?
Three. How do I pace myself so that I arrive on time?
Two. Can I remember the way, or must I keep glancing at the map?
One. Do I have to go the same way every time?

Ignition . . . We have power.

It's a clean liftoff—and another sermon is on its way to a divinely appointed rendezvous—a carefully chosen destination that will meet needs of the passengers on board.

It's a good thing the pilot knows what to do. The passengers are counting on that expertise for this journey of discovery. On this trip they will find treasure greater than silver or gold. This pilot-pastor will conduct them toward an encounter with Jesus Christ in his Word. The passengers' confidence in their pilot is strong. Most travel with him at least once a week. Sunday morning comes, and they strap themselves in for another ride. Lately, though, there have been a few empty seats on board. Some have begun dozing through most of the trip. And, to be honest, the pilot-pastor has been thinking about transferring to a new assignment—maybe even a different kind of job—something down on the ground where it's safe.

You may be that pastor. You may be ready to turn in your wings—hang it up and let some other sap handle your ship. Trouble is, you keep hearing that little voice, the one that called you to be a pilot in the first place. The Holy Spirit might just want you to read this book. He called us to write it. We've designed it to keep you flying.

If your preaching seems grounded we want to help get you back into the air. If you are a first-time flyer this flight manual will walk through the steps toward sermon preparation, and the first three chapters will provide some basic training. But most of this book focuses on the sermon itself. We want you to know how to package your material for maximum impact.

One of the main features of our book is the flight plan for a sermon—a communication model of what a sermon looks like. The model is shown in Appendix B and discussed on pages 176–85. The design is less imposing than that of a rocket flight; in fact the metaphor moves from aeronautics to archery. And it is more realistic to your setting and resources. We have found it helpful in our preaching and teaching to picture the sermon as an arrow flying toward the target bull's-eye. The arrow comes out of its quiver in chapter 3.

The basics

There are four basic requirements of every sermon: You must be accurate, clear, relevant, and interesting.

Accuracy

If you, as the pilot-pastor, are going to transport your people from point A to point B spiritually, if your purpose is transformation rather than mere information, then your sermon must first be accurate. You can't say "thus sayeth the Lord," if the Lord hasn't thus said. We must know what the text says and be able to express it exegetically and theologically before we dare package it homiletically.

Careful attention to accuracy also helps make sure the applications you select are valid, arising out of the text in its context. To impose an application on a text builds a house on sand; it just won't stand up over time, let alone offer eternal truth. We must understand our text exegetically and theologically before we can apply it with legitimacy.

Accuracy depends on disciplined practice of study and prayer. Study we can handle. But if we aren't careful, study by itself can leave us feeling pretty smug. Isn't it great that we are so humble, considering how much we know?

But there is another potential problem as well—a problem for the congregation. An accurate, well-studied message can be an abstract, disembodied, and lifeless piece of pedantry if it is divorced from prayer. As Lewis Sperry Chafer used to say, "You can be clear as ice—and just as cold!" Prayer is the fire God uses to warm up a message and thaw a frozen heart. You should not think of serving a raw sermon to your congregation any more than you would serve raw steak to your dinner guests. Only the fire of prayer makes a sermon sizzle. We cover basic exegetical and theological spadework, plus prayer, in chapters 1 and 2.

Relevance

Once you understand a text you have to understand the audience. Chapter 3 prepares a preacher to discover a passage's relevance to a people's needs so truth can be applied to the bumps and scrapes that afflict human hearts. Find out what the text says. That will narrow the options considerably when you point truth to meet specific needs. Then explore how what the text says applies to your audience in particular. This step will help define the purpose for your sermon and the motivation for your congregation to apply the message. The purpose keeps you on target, focused on life change.

Clarity

Part 2 (chaps. 4–6) explores different facets of clarity and interest and how they may be used to build the introduction, body, and conclusion. We largely determine the value of a diamond by its clarity. The same goes for a sermon. If it is not clear, not only will it fail to shine, but it won't be worth much. What does it matter how accurate we are in exegesis if we fail to communicate that truth clearly?

Chapter 4 moves the sermon onto its launch pad: the introduction. A good introduction acquaints the audience with the text, uncovering need and raising interest. Start out right, and you have a much better chance of ending where you want to be. A raw rump roast isn't that appetizing, but throw it on a hot grill and suddenly—hunger! This chapter shows you how to make people hungry for God's Word.

Chapter 5 looks at the second stage of sermon structure: the body and its transitions. The body comprises two or more points, but each part should flow into the next with barely a ripple at the confluence. Movement should be logical, even *necessary*. The key to fluid movement between parts is a good transition. A good transition is like a navigational compass. You use it to remind your congregation of where you've been and where you are going. Transitions also enhance clarity as they reveal the simple logic of the argument or the unfolding of the story.

Interest

Transitions link, but they also help move the message forward. They help maintain interest as they highlight the tension among points of a sermon, priming the listener for what comes next. In this way transitions work as a gear shift. Gears are essential to a car's ability to move from one town to the next, yet gears by themselves aren't much help. You need to be able to shift from gear to gear. Transitions shift gears in a sermon. We will take transitions apart and see how they can help a sermon develop smoothly and move forward.

In chapter 6 we learn how to structure the conclusion. Purpose keeps the sermon focused on its application; the conclusion keeps the preacher focused on how structure brings the application to life. The purpose captivates the heart. The conclusion magnetizes the mind. The sermon's *purpose* passionately embraces God's truth, setting the emotional stage for a Romeo-and-Juliet encounter with the Holy Spirit. The *conclusion* reinforces that purpose. *Together* they should make life change a matter of the heart— a longing for God.

Once you start the manuscript, the conclusion draws the rest of the sermon logically and structurally to itself. You notice how, when a nail and a magnet decide they're made for each other, the path of the nail as it moves toward the magnet does not meander. A powerful conclusion, carefully outlined, keeps the sermon from wandering off course. It enables you to fulfil your purpose with precision.

Section 3 (chaps. 7–8) takes a "squinch-eyed" look at how to sustain interest once you have it. Your parishioners have signed up for a sermon trip week after week; you want them to be with you in more than body. Chapter 7 is the fun chapter since it helps with gathering support materials. Where do you find them? Which are the best kinds?

What about a filing system in which I can really find the stuff I need?[1]

In chapter 8 we resurrect the art of style. Careful word choice has never been more important than in this age of the one–word paragraph. The English language has become sound–bitten and media–mangled to capitalize on the decreasing attention spans of the "Nintendo generation." We simply cannot afford to waste verbal ammunition as we choose and load words carefully into a manuscript for maximum effect in spiritual warfare.

In section 4 we chart the trip so that your fellow travelers will remain interested from week to week. For example, what about pace in a sermon? How do you get it out of first gear? Should we pop the clutch, peel out, burn rubber, hit cruising speed, and then coast? How do you know when to speed up and when to slow down? How much time should you spend on each point before shifting to the next? Learning to pace your sermon so that it has a sense of climax will add variety to your delivery and effectiveness to your message. That's in chapter nine.

Chapter 10 shows you how to preach without notes so you can use your eyes for more important things. Ask yourself, "Whom do I enjoy visiting with more, someone who looks me in the eye or someone who is always distracted?" That doesn't mean you memorize your manuscript. A sermon can remember itself. Our model shows you how.

In chapter 11 we show how to plan sermons so you don't have to travel the same way every time. Every sermon need not be a rocket ride. You are free to change vehicles

1. Developing a usable filing system, and then using it, is one of the most important things a preacher can do. Since most of us aren't all that organized by nature we need help, and one of the best resources we have found is Michael P. Green's *Green's Filing Systems: For Pastors and Christian Workers* (Grand Rapids: Baker, 1991). The great thing about this book is that the author explains different types of filing methods and shows how to find and set up the one that is best for you personally.

from week to week. One sermon might be more like a leisurely stroll down a deductive golf course fairway, where the view is panoramic and the destination in sight from the first tee. Another might resemble an African safari with a perilous inductive trail. Listeners must shadow your every step, uncertain of the destination but fascinated by the trip. The scenery is equally impressive on a variety of trips, and all can reach the necessary destination. The subject and the audience's needs will help you decide the kind of trip you want to take.

Words of fire and ice

Putting sermons together for such vivid impact is hard work, but the result will be worth it. Your investment of time and energy will, by God's grace, yield a congregation that has been moved (and not merely shaken) through your preaching. In the process of working through this material you will rediscover a joy and freedom in your preaching where perhaps you were feeling a bit stale and bound. You can use these ideas to strike sparks in your sermons—the kind of sparks that will rekindle the fire you thought had gone out. We want to help you fan those sparks into a flame, to produce the kind of fire that our Lord is fond of using to thaw hearts and transform enemies into sons and daughters.

But this book isn't just about verbal pyrotechnics. It's about getting the Word inside again where it burns in the heart of a pastor who, in turn, burns for his God and his God's people. It's about how God can use a sermon to transform points of view into points of vision, the metamorphosis of belief into conviction. It's about the igneous stuff of sermons that God can use to make a life incandescent. It's about the words that flow out of that kind of heart—words of fire *and* ice, sand *and* rain; words that rip like a Texas tornado and caress like a summer breeze. It's about having a destination for every sermon and getting there on time.

This book is about how to preach a sermon filled with God's power from God's Word in God's strength.

We don't want to forget those who have helped us in this project. In a real sense this has been a team effort. Haddon W. Robinson first sparked our desire to soar to the homiletical heights. Thanks, Haddon. Those were good years we spent learning from you.

Where can the list stop after that? Sam Canine, Bill Lawrence, Duane Litfin, Eugene Lowry, Calvin Miller, Calvin Pearson, Tim Ralston, Don Regier, Ramesh Richard, Don Sunukjian, Timothy Warren, to name but a few. Syd Field's creative insight, discovered in *Screenplay*,[2] helped us see the possibility for *power sermon* models.

Scores of students at Dallas Theological Seminary have tried out our ideas and helped us reshape and correct. The wonderful congregations at Stryker, Ohio, and Sherman, Texas, the faithful believers of the Ohio and Texas Air National Guard, and friends in many parts of the world have encouraged and challenged us. Special thanks go to our wives Lauren and Erris for their loving encouragement, inspiration, and patience.

As authors we invite further comment on the effectiveness of the power sermon model. If you have questions or are willing to share an experience, positive or negative, write to us at Dallas Seminary, 3909 Swiss Avenue, Dallas, TX 75204.

2. Syd Field, ed., *Screenplay: The Foundations of Screenwriting*, rev. ed. (New York: Dell, 1984).

Part 1
Obtaining the Fuel

1

Mining the Ore: Exegesis, Subjects, and Complements

What Is the Sermon about?

T minus eleven.

In the exegetical step our goal is accuracy.

Most of us who preach want to vault from the Bible to the sermon. Too often we climb into the cockpit and take off without much concern for where we are going, or how we will get there. Just get out of the way and let us preach. We want to fly!

This desire to preach before we've done our homework is a sore temptation we must resist. We simply must be sure of what God's Word says. In order to be sure we need to dig. Before we soar into the homiletical heavens we need to mine the ore for the fuel. Then we need to build the rocket and design a flight plan that will carry us to a particular destination.

So put on your miner's hard hat and let's begin by digging into the text.

How do we know where to begin? I know I'm looking for truth, but where do I start? To continue the ore analogy, the exegete may feel like a miner standing on a mountain. Inside, somewhere, is a rich vein of gold, so the miner digs from the top down. That miner may reach the gold eventually, but enormous time and energy resources will be wasted. The hard working miner may wind up holding fool's gold and even be tempted, after so much investment in the search, to pass it off as the genuine item.

The miner needs a map—a step-by-step guide to the treasure.

The first chapters of this book construct a sort of treasure map. We will outline the way clearly. Follow and the treasure is yours for the taking. It's a rather unusual map. You can use it over and over, follow the same steps, and discover a different treasure every time. Exegetical study and theological refining are essential for developing a good sermon.[1]

The first two steps—exegesis and theology—keep us honest by disciplining us to accurately handle God's Word. This is no game. Our interpretation of the biblical text may be used by the Holy Spirit to shape the eternal destinies of those who hear our words. Chapter 2 will discuss theology; this chapter stops at the spot on the treasure map marked by an "X"—for eXegesis.

Exegesis

Accuracy in exegesis is a goal we aim for, but not the prize itself. A great sermon must be more than accurate, but it can never be less. An accurate message reveals

1. For excellent studies of the exposition process, see Haddon W. Robinson, *Biblical Preaching* (Grand Rapids: Baker, 1980); Duane Litfin, *Public Speaking: A Handbook for Christians*, 2d ed. (Grand Rapids: Baker, 1992); Henry Grady Davis, *Design for Preaching* (Philadelphia: Fortress, 1958), and Timothy Warren, "A Paradigm for Preaching," *Bibliotheca Sacra*, 148.592 (October–December 1991): 424–41.

God's message to his people. Its authority comes from his Word. The preacher serves simply as messenger. This authority invites a congregation to press confidently toward maturity. You won't be dragging them along at the end of a leash.

There is no glory in this first step. It is a time to roll up sleeves and slog through by torch light—and lots of prayer. Prayer is your investment by faith. You are committed to the transforming work of the Spirit through his Word. You are willing to pay the price to make sure your sermon, the trip you chart for your people on a Sunday morning, is accurate.

Before you begin digging into the text ask two questions:

1. Have I prayed that the Lord would help me understand his Word?
2. Have I mentally isolated the text under consideration from my audience?

Have I prayed for understanding?

Let's consider the first question. If you haven't prayed, then you aren't prepared to begin. We who teach God's Word need to remind ourselves constantly of our utter dependence on the Holy Spirit to guide us and to illumine our minds.

First Corinthians 2:10–13 encourages us that the deep truth of God can be revealed only by the Spirit of God to the child of God. God's Spirit differs essentially from the spirit of the world. The spirit of the world whispers that if we only study hard enough, if we only dig deeply enough, we will eventually mine the deep things of God. While digging is necessary, it will profit us nothing if we work in darkness. We may as well not have begun at all. God's Spirit is like the lamp on our helmets that reveals the precious ore. We must ask his help if we are to extract gold.

Have I "isolated" the text?

The second question seems strange: "Have I mentally isolated the text under consideration from my audience?" I thought I was supposed to be preparing this message for my congregation.

That's true, but to ensure that we give the most accurate interpretation of the text, so that we do not read into it something that isn't there, we need to interpret the text free from outside influences. If I think about my audience and their needs now, I may unintentionally color a precise interpretation of what Moses or David or Paul had to say. I must understand exactly what meaning the author had to convey to his audience before I can understand what God wants me to say to mine.

Isolate the text and you free the Spirit to reveal truths you might never see if you impose the needs of specific individuals on to the passage. As we consider the text by itself, let's switch gears for a minute. Rather than picturing a mining expedition, try thinking of the text as a building. Considering the needs of your audience too early is like using a crowbar, forcing the passage to move in a way that is unnatural. Eventually you may dismantle its unity and integrity. Then you are left with an exegetical shambles, fit for nothing but kindling.

Steps along the path of exegesis

Question the text

You want to take a measuring tape to the text, not a crowbar. Measuring tapes are objective. They don't impose values. They record them. Find out how the book you are preaching is constructed. Use your exegetical tape to make sure your measurements are precise and accurate:

> For what purpose was this book, this "building," originally designed?

What objectives did the original author/architect have in
   mind to fulfil the purpose?

In tone, grammar and structure, would you liken this
   book to a toolshed (Romans), a woodshed (1 Corinthians), a king's palace (Matthew), a train station
   (Mark), or a honeymoon cottage (Song of Solomon)?

Each preaching passage may be compared to a room or
hallway in that building. These pieces should all fit together to meet the specific criteria of the biblical author and
the needs of his audience. Once you see the whole building, then you can get down to a detailed study of the room
where your sermon lives.

The immediate challenge is to measure a preaching passage by studying and interpreting all its parts. This is the inductive part of our study—looking at all the parts in order
to make sense of the whole. Begin by reading a passage
through several times in the context of its chapter. As time
allows, read through the entire book to get an idea of how
the passage fits into the overall design. The greater mastery you have of the whole book, the more fully you will
understand your passage.

As you read, take notes on significant details. "Significant details" would include notes on:

Who? ... Who wrote the book? To whom was it
   addressed?

What? ... What is the situation? What is being encouraged or discouraged?

When? ... When was this book penned?

Where? ... Where do the recipients of this book live?

Why? ... Why are these commands given?

How? ... How are Christians expected to respond to
   this truth?

Don't neglect to write down any questions that may come to your mind. Remember, if you don't understand what a word or concept means chances are your audience won't either! Take time to look it up and find out what it means.

Outline the text

Now use all the measurements (exegetical observations) to compose a full sentence outline. Phrase outlines don't count, for fragmented writing is nothing but fragmented thinking on paper. At this point you are writing in a historical vein, thinking through what Jesus said, what Paul encouraged, how the readers were to respond. . . . Check out your conclusions against commentaries.

As an exercise read through Matthew 15:1–28 a couple of times. Then consider the following outline. Note that each sentence is declarative. There are no questions, nor are there any imperatives in an exegetical outline:

An Exegetical Outline of Matthew 15:1–28

I. (15:1–20) Jesus reveals that the Pharisees are not in right relationship with God because they have made traditions more important than God's commandments.
   A. (15:1–2) The Pharisees accuse Jesus of violating the tradition of the elders.
   B. (15:3–9) Jesus condemns the Pharisees for setting aside the Word of God for the sake of their tradition.
   C. (15:10–20) Jesus explains to his followers that the Pharisees judge an individual's righteousness by external adherence to a set of rules, rather than by the internal state of the heart.
      1. (15:10–11) Jesus explains to the multitude that it is not what comes from the outside that defiles, but what comes from the inside.
      2. (15:12–14) Jesus explains to his disciples that they should have nothing to do with the Pharisees, whose future condemnation is secure.

3. (15:15–20) Jesus explains to Peter that the evils that proceed out of a heart defile a person in the sight of God, not the outside appearances with which the Pharisees are concerned.

II. (15:21–28) Jesus applauds the right relationship of a Canaanite woman to God by responding positively to her great faith.
   A. (15:21–22) The Canaanite woman approaches Jesus as the Jewish Messiah, asking that he heal her demon possessed daughter.
   B. (15:23–24) Jesus refuses to acknowledge her.
   C. (15:25) The woman asks a second time, approaching not as to a Jew but rather acknowledging Jesus' lordship over her life.
   D. (15:26) Jesus challenges her request on the basis that she is a Gentile.
   E. (15:27) The woman responds in humility and faith.
   F. (15:28) Jesus applauds her faith and grants her request.

Frame a propositional statement

Now comes the hard part: Condense the outline into a precise propositional statement.

That central proposition comprises two distinct parts: (1) the *subject*, or what the author is talking about; (2) the *complement*, or what the author says about what he is talking about.

What is the author saying to his audience? What is he talking about? The answer to this question is called the *exegetical subject*. Consider Matthew 15:1–28.[2] By looking at the exegetical observations I have made from this passage I understand that Matthew is contrasting a wrong relationship to God (the Pharisees') with a right relationship to God (the Canaanite woman's). The Pharisees seem to

2. Matt. 15:1–28 will serve as our case study throughout this book. For maximum benefit readers might wish to select another passage to work out, perhaps from an Epistle.

think they can obtain righteousness before God by keeping human traditions. They are concerned with external marks of righteousness.

The Canaanite woman discovers that she can have a right relationship with God only if her heart responds to him in faith. She is concerned with internal righteousness. Jesus denounces the Pharisees and commends the woman, answering her prayer for her daughter. Phrase the subject as a question:

> What does Jesus teach the Jewish Pharisees and a Gentile woman concerning a right relationship with God?

Now turn that subject into an incomplete phrase. Try answering one of the six focusing questions to narrow the subject: *Who? What? When? Where? Why? How?* You could use the same questions to help you focus your outline points as well. In Matthew 15 it looks as if Jesus is addressing *how* to have a right relationship with God. Our exegetical subject then might look something like this:

> Exegetical subject: What Jesus teaches the Jewish Pharisees and a Gentile woman concerning how to have a right relationship with God . . .

Sounds technical, historical, nonrelational, right? Exactly. The exegetical subject takes the text as it is and reflects the structure and emphasis of the biblical writer to his audience in the most precise language possible.

Now we are ready to answer the question that helped us form the exegetical subject phrase. The answer will be our complement. The relationship between the subject and complement is the relationship between a question (the subject) and an answer (the complement).

The question was, "What does Jesus teach the Jewish Pharisees and a Gentile woman concerning how to have a right relationship with God?" The answer for Matthew 15:1–20 would look something like this:

> Complement: not by keeping religious rules, but by responding to Christ in faith.

We could also think of the relationship of subject to complement as a marriage. The second half of the central proposition "complements" or "completes" the subject, much as Eve complemented Adam; she made up for what was lacking in him. The marriage of the subject and complement form the central proposition, which is stated as a declarative sentence:

> Exegetical central proposition: Jesus teaches the Jewish Pharisees and a Gentile woman that a right relationship with God is not established by keeping religious rules, but by responding to Christ in faith.

Establish the text's purpose

Now that we have a good idea of what the text is saying we need to ask other questions:

Why is this text placed in this particular context?
What is the purpose of this text?
Is the author trying to get his readers to start doing something (exhortation), to stop doing something (warning), or to continue doing something (encouragement)?
In what way is this text designed to change a person's attitudes and/or actions?
What does the author want his audience to believe more strongly, feel more deeply, or do more readily?"

In this particular passage we discover the purpose that is common to all of God's Word: *transformation.* What kind of life change did Matthew wish to see in his audience? A study of the text in it's context reveals the exegetical purpose of Matthew 15:1–28 might be to encourage a right relationship with God by condemning the self-sufficient attitude of the Pharisees and by applauding the Gentile woman's attitude of humble dependence in worship.

A point of danger

Congratulations! You have completed the first major step in preparing a sermon. Now we are ready to forge ahead. Let's return to the picture of our mining expedition. The climb has been tough, but you are determined to see it through. Just on the other side of the mountain a delightful homiletical paradise beckons. There apples of gold glitter in settings of silver. The aroma of truth mingled with the delicious scent of style drifts over the mountain top to wrap you in its spell. You could almost float up and over to that beautiful valley. You catch the sound of music on the breeze, music once familiar but now, almost unrecognizable and all the more intoxicating for its rarity—the harmony of passion and integrity. There, on the other side of the mountain. Just out of reach.

But the lure of a finished sermon is so strong. Maybe you could take a shortcut—the treacherous trail around the mountain that separates exegesis from homiletics. It's a sheer drop to the bottom. But, you say to yourself that you are a gifted climber. If you are careful you might be able to carry this heavy ore to your people and trust God to help them convert it for practical use. That's what most preachers do, isn't it? Carry the burden of exegesis directly to the people, dump it on them and then ask God to apply it to their hearts? Many have tried, it's true. . . .

Peering over the edge of your exegetical ledge, down through the mists to the very bottom of the mountain, you

see a society of thin preachers exhorting thin congregations. These are the ones who tried to jump from exegesis
to homiletics and fell far short of their goal. They never
even got close to true homiletics, because they wanted to
skip the harder uphill climb through the theological thick-
ets. And so they fell—down into the valley of starved sermons; down into flatlands of two-dimensional truth. It's a
land of pretty homilies where smoke and mirrors can trick
a congregation into believing a sermon has theological
depth, when in fact it's a thin shadow.

It's a scary place to live, this land where you can never
be sure of the truth of your message. Down in the valley
you can focus on one preacher who knows the message
is weak and invalid, incapable of standing on it's own. It
needs some "help." So the preacher dresses it up in fancy
homiletical phrases and parades it for others to admire.
It's a pathetic sight. Oh, not that it isn't nice. Not that the
preacher's motives aren't pure, and the words, along
with all the other words that float up from the valley, are
lovely.

But they ring hollow. These are fragile sermons, quickly
produced, quickly admired, quickly forgotten, designed to
cleanse the soul but unable to scrub away the sin. Like a
pretty soap bubble the message contains all the elements
for cleansing. It just isn't substantive enough to get the job
done.

You remind yourself, "Good motives don't make a good
message." That's not the place for you. Yours is the higher
road. The road to theological truth. You turn toward the
next plateau and you discover a theological bridge. You
are hesitant—this bridge has not been crossed by many
preachers recently. But it's the only way, and you decide to
cross over to the next stop on the path to a good sermon.

Never fear; you won't have to go alone. We'll cross the
bridge together and move on to the next plateau in
chapter 2.

Chapter summary:

Exegesis, subjects, and complements

1. Pray first for insight into God's Word.
2. Determine to discover the biblical author's meaning and audience.
3. Read through the passage several times in different versions.
4. Do an inductive study of the passage in its context.
5. Develop an exegetical outline, following the flow of the passage.
6. Posit an exegetical subject and complement.
7. Join the exegetical subject and complement to form the exegetical central proposition.
8. Discover the textual purpose based on the central proposition.

2

Refining the Ore: Theology

What Does the Rest of the Bible Say about My Proposition?

T minus ten.

We continue to purify our accuracy.

You are about to enter a neglected but rich realm of study on your way to a great sermon. Back at the exegetical step we unearthed raw exegetical ore. Now we want to refine it into a pure theological statement. Preachers are bedrock theologians. They build the core of the sermon on the solid rock of theology. You are likely the most famous theologian your congregation knows.

Is it really necessary to take this theological step? Yes, because it sharpens your knowledge of theological truth and because this theological step serves to check initial exegetical conclusions and to confirm interpretive decisions. Sounds like work, doesn't it? Stick with it! Good things come from hard work and concentrated effort.

Many families like to put together large picture puzzles. At first the task looks hopeless—so many pieces. We start at the corners and sides to get an outline of the picture. Then we fill in the middle. Slowly we study each piece of that scene to see where it might fit to make something beautiful. One of the keys to success in reconstructing a beautiful scene from jumbled pieces is patience.

Little children are the most impatient. They want to skip the work of experimenting with different angles to try to see how pieces relate. They would go from pieces to picture and forget the puzzle part. So they try to force pieces that *almost* fit, and the result is a mess. It's a picture all right, but nothing like what the designer intended.

Seeing the big (theological) picture

The words of the text in their context are like pieces of a jumbled puzzle. Exegesis allows us to see individual pieces and how they might fit. Theology makes sure we do not force pieces together unnaturally. There is a pattern, a natural design, to the truths of the Bible. Sometimes we have to study a piece of truth for a long time before we see how it fits into the big picture of God's revelation.

We can't afford to be impatient. The stakes are too high; this puzzle contains a message that may alter the course of a life. If we don't get it right—if we start forcing truths together unnaturally—then we risk getting (and giving) the wrong message. Take as much time as you need to see how the exegetical pieces fit together to suggest a theological principle. Getting the big picture, figuring out the puzzle, is hard work. It takes concentrated effort. But the outcome, a sermon of beauty and truth that God can use to change a life, is worth the sweat.

The hard work of doing theology comes after we crack the exegetical nut. Exegesis will reveal a historical application of a timeless theological principle. Sometimes the theological principle and the exegetical proposition are virtually identical. Some go down easily:

Exegetical proposition: God forbade Israel to steal.
Theological principle: God forbids stealing.

Others are like swallowing thorns:

Exegetical proposition: Paul encouraged women to submit to male leadership in the church.
Theological principle: Women are to submit to male leadership in the worshiping community.

Sometimes cultural differences raise interpretive challenges:

Exegetical proposition: Paul encouraged the Corinthian believers to exercise love by giving up their right to eat meat sacrificed to idols if it might cause another Christian to sin.
Theological principle: Love limits liberty.

Instances such as the last one, in which we are separated from the cultural expression of the principle, make us dig harder to make sure the principle we derive is legitimate. Meat sacrificed to idols is no longer a problem. There are, however, analogous relationships or cultural equivalents. What is the equivalent of meat sacrificed to an idol in our culture? The danger in seeking cultural equivalents is that there are no controls on which elements I decide need emphasis. We easily slide into allegorical interpretation. That's when we discover significance in insignificant objects, actions, or people. Suddenly the stones of the well in Samaria in John 4 are symbolic of the hardness of the woman's heart. The stones of the well are only supporting players in the story of Jesus encounter with the Samaritan woman. They were never meant to take center stage.

Find the principles

Look for the principle first. That theological principle will give you the needed focus to help you consider which elements in the story require parallel development once you get to homiletics. For example, regarding the theological principle "Love limits liberty" from 1 Corinthians 8, I might ask myself, "What Christian liberty might I need to forsake to help a brother or sister not sin?" Drinking alcohol may come to mind, or hugging members of the opposite sex in public.

All of these are, of course, culturally equivalent to offering meat sacrificed to idols, but we discovered them in an orderly way by considering the theological principle rather than by arbitrarily choosing which of the exegetical elements we ought to highlight. By looking at the principle first we discovered the main parallel we can apply: It is an unselfish action to give up a right for the sake of a weaker brother or sister. The focus, then, is on action rather than on the specific "piece of meat" we need to give up.

Try thinking of the relationship between exegesis and theology this way: Exegesis is the parent, and theology is the child. The *exegetical outline, exegetical central proposition,* and the *exegetical purpose* give birth to the *theological outline, theological central proposition,* and *theological purpose.* Theology grows out of exegesis. That is why the theological step follows the exegetical step.

As in the exegetical step, the theological outline comes first, then the theological central proposition, and finally the theological purpose statement. Remember to express all theological content in a way that is universal or timeless; the points of the outline, the central proposition, and the purpose statement should apply to people in any society, place, and age.

The material will emerge purely theological, untainted by cultural influences. If you can restrict the points of the outline, the central proposition or the purpose statement to any particular historical era, then you may be facing one of two problems: First, you may not state the truth broadly enough. Second, your observation may not be a universal principle. Pure theological truth transcends culture and time. Avoid historically limiting references to "church," "Israel," "Christians," "Moses," "the Ephesians," or "the Pharisees." Rather, use "believers" (believers inhabit any age), "unbelievers," "people," and other timeless references. Don't tie the statement down to any time.

The theological bridge stretches before us. Pick up your exegetical outline, central proposition, and purpose, and off you go. As you cross the bridge two theological questions about your passage must be answered:

1. What does this passage say about God, his creation, and the relationship between God and his creation?[1]
2. How do these timeless truths fit into what the rest of the Bible says on this subject?

We need to ask the first question of the exegetical outline, of the exegetical central proposition, and of the exegetical purpose. The answers will give the biblical theology of this author in this book concerning this truth.

Form a theological outline

It's important to question the theological content of every point in the exegetical outline because we want the theological outline to be just that—theological rather than exegetical. Questioning every exegetical point eliminates historically time-bound material. In most cases a theological outline will be shorter than the exegetical outline. Not every exegetical detail expresses a theological principle.

1. Timothy Warren, "A Paradigm for Preaching," *Bibliotheca Sacra*, 148.592 (October–December 1991): 424–41.

In other words, don't use an exegetical brick to build a theological house. If your exegetical point doesn't reveal a timeless theological principle, then go on to the next point with a clear conscience.

In the following theological outline of Matthew 15:1–28 each point is expressed as a principle. Again, please note: Only declarative sentences should be in a theological outline:

A Theological Outline of Matthew 15:1–28

I. (15:1–20) People will never have a right relationship with God as long as they trust in their own ability to make the relationship right.
   A. Prideful self-sufficiency may prompt those who think they can earn God's favor through good works to view moral defilement as something that comes from outside rather than inside.
   B. Emphasis on outward conformity to religious rules reveals a trust in personal self-righteousness to have a right relationship with God.
      1. An attitude of self-sufficiency leads to spiritual blindness.
      2. Spiritual blindness leads to God's condemnation.

II. (15:21–28) People will only have a right relationship with God when they place their faith in God's ability to make the relationship right.
   A. Prideful self-sufficiency may prompt those who believe that God is impressed by flattery to seek a right relationship with God based on outward appearance.
   B. God can break through the barrier of self-sufficiency to encourage people to humble themselves before him.
   C. God readily extends his grace to anyone who bows before him with a humble heart.
      1. A right relationship with God begins with a right understanding of who God is.

2. A right understanding of who God is will be followed by recognition of personal inability and a
   humble acknowledgment of need.

Identify the theological subject

Now that we have seen the parts as related principles
we need to question the exegetical central proposition:
*What does this passage as a whole have to say about God,
his creation, and the relationship between God and his
creation?* The answer will give the theological subject.
This theological subject need not be stated as a complete
sentence for it is a general statement of subject, as is the
case for our theological subject for Matthew 15:

> Theological subject: How people (creation) can have a
> right relationship with God (the relationship between
> God and his creation).

Add the complement

To find the complement ask what the author says about
this subject. How *does* Matthew answer the question of
how people can have a right relationship with God? Remember, the answer to the question (the subject) will give
us the complement. The answer might be:

> . . . by recognizing personal insufficiency and by placing
> faith in God's sufficiency.

Contrast the exegetical central proposition and the
theological central proposition for Matthew 15: 1–28 (Note
that both are declarative sentences):

> Exegetical central proposition: Jesus teaches the Jewish
> Pharisees and a Gentile woman that they cannot estab-
> lish a right relationship with God by keeping religious
> rules; they must respond to Christ in faith.

Theological central proposition: People obtain a right relationship with God by recognizing personal insufficiency
and by placing faith in God's sufficiency.

The theological central proposition differs from the exegetical central proposition in three major aspects:

1. A theological central proposition is abstract; an exegetical central proposition tends to be concrete.
2. A theological central proposition is broad; an exegetical central proposition is specific.
3. A theological central proposition is timeless; an exegetical central proposition is bound to the biblical
   time.

Discover the theological purpose statement

The theological purpose statement flows out of the
theological central proposition. State it as a universal principle. In formulating the theological purpose statement
you want to ask what universal principle was in the author's mind and behind the author's purpose. When you
unearth that principle you have discovered your theological purpose statement, which, in the case of Matthew 15:1–
28, might be:

Theological purpose statement: To encourage people to
seek a right relationship with God by revealing their personal insufficiency and their need to place faith in God's
sufficiency.

Notice that the purpose is expressed in universal or
timeless terms. It is to encourage *people* rather than the
Pharisees, or the Syrophoenician woman. Also, the word
people embraces both believers and unbelievers; the principle applies to both.

Now that you have discovered what the parts of this passage have to say about God, his creation and the relationship between the two, you are half way across the theological bridge. Keep pushing ahead in the strength of his Spirit. Remember, this work is by him, of him and for him, so take a minute to rededicate this sermon to the Lord. Now that you have your second wind, let's move across the second half.

Already we have discovered universal, timeless truths in this passage and expressed them in the form of a preliminary theological outline, theological central proposition, and theological purpose statement. Your first stab at these theological principles is preliminary because so far we have only discovered what we believe to be the biblical theology of this author in this book.

Bring all of Scripture to bear

That is really a narrow slice. Surely the rest of the Bible has something to add. Just to make sure our principles agree with the whole counsel of God, let's check them against the rest of Scripture. We now need to ask the second major theological question: *How do these timeless truths fit into what the rest of the Bible says on this subject?*

Test each principle expressed in the theological outline, central proposition and purpose statement against the whole testimony of Scripture. This need not be a detailed analysis. As you search the Bible on the subject, simply ask yourself two basic questions: First, does Scripture ever contradict your interpretation of this author? Second, does Scripture support or enhance your interpretation?

If you find that your theology conflicts with the clear teaching of other Scripture then you need to reconsider your interpretation of the text. If your findings agree with or complement other biblical teachings on this subject you can proceed with confidence.

This important step will uncover the author's contribution to systematic theology and so enhance your own appreciation for the unity of Scripture. Also, you will correct and/or verify your preliminary theological interpretation. Your assurance, your confidence, and the authority with which you preach will increase proportionately.

In the case of Matthew 15:1–28 all the points in this outline, proposition, and purpose agree with other biblical teachings on this subject. Also, they reflect the unique message of Matthew in precise and timeless terms—just as each facet of a diamond reflects the light that strikes it in a way that contributes to the brilliance of the whole gem.

Since our theological outline, central proposition, and purpose stood the test of the second theological question, they can remain unchanged.

Conclusion

In chapter 1 you discovered the structure (the exegetical outline) and essence (the exegetical central proposition) of what Matthew was saying to his audience. In chapter 2 you derived from the exegetical data universal principles, which you have expressed in the form of a theological outline, theological proposition, and theological purpose.

Now for some good news. It's treasure time! You are ready to construct the sermon to meet the needs of your audience. But what are their needs? If your message doesn't speak to their needs, they may not agree that what you have found is a treasure at all. And how can you build a sermon that will meet those needs once you discover what they are? We'll find out in chapter 3.

Chapter summary:

Theology

1. Pray for insight into the text's universal principles.

2. Discover the biblical theology of the author in the text.
3. Submit the author's theology to the more comprehensive discipline of systematic theology.
4. Express the flow of the author's argument in a theological outline.
5. Express the theological principle in the form of a timeless, universal subject and complement.
6. Join theological subject and complement to form the theological central proposition.
7. Discover the theological purpose, based on the theological central proposition.

3

Developing the Fuel: Proposition, Purpose, and Destination

Where Is the Sermon Going?

T minus nine.

In the homiletical step we aim at relevancy.

You have the refined ore in your hand—truth. Through your diligence and the Holy Spirit's illuminating work you understand the theology of the passage and how that timeless truth applied to the original readers. Your heart and mind holds a priceless, timeless gift of life-changing truth. You are about to carry it home to your people.

Preparing to leave the rarefied atmosphere of a high theological plateau you gaze out on a vast plain at the foot of the mountain. There, on the same level as the biblical audience is your congregation, waiting for a word from God that will bring them into closer communion, deeper fellowship, and a more consistent walk with their Lord. Instinctively you want to run to them with the treasure you

43

have found, like Moses bringing the Word of God down from Mount Sinai. More than anything, you want to feed his lambs, enriching their souls with this imperishable gift.

But wait. Your audience lives in townhouses and tenements, not tents, and you don't look a thing like Charlton Heston. Thousands of years separate them from those who first discovered this treasure. For that first audience, God's commands were immediately and obviously relevant.

What do your people have to do with Pharisaical traditions and the prejudices that separated Jews from Samaritans? Matthew had a particular audience in mind, as did the rest of the biblical writers. They wrote to particular needs with specific purposes. The first readers didn't have to go through the process of distilling the theological essence of God's message first, because it was immediately applicable to their situation. It was tailor fit to their culture and time.

So here you stand, doubtfully reconsidering a pocketful of timeless truths. All the labor of extraction has yielded, it seems, only bloodless abstractions—theological principles fit to no particular purpose. Here is truth, yes, but so what? By dissecting the text you have gained knowledge of what made the text tick, but the biblical operation has become an autopsy, and now you are left holding a homiletical corpse.

You dare not invite people to cross the chasm and join you on the theological plain. Who wants to view a dissected body of truth (regardless of how well it was done)? Most could not delight in these rather antiseptic truths any more than we would delight in seeing a butchered cow. We would much rather have the sizzling steak properly seasoned, without knowing how the steak got there.

We must reassemble this body of truth in a recognizable form to take people beyond knowledge of how this truth changed the lives of the original listeners to how it can change their lives. They must become participants in the cosmic drama, not mere observers of God at work on a two thousand year old stage. How do these principles bear on their lives, filling their hearts as well as their heads? This chapter is all about motivating as well as informing. We want to explore how to reveal the relevancy of God's Word to a particular congregation. To do that we need to cross another bridge.

Tailor words to meet needs

To meet particular needs you must know what those needs are. That means you need to know people—analyze them. Are they primarily white-collar or blue-collar? Are there many working mothers? Single-parent homes? Latchkey kids? What is the educational and cultural level of these people? What primary recreational activities (secular and Christian) are available for children and adults? In short, what are the demographic data for these people? This is no small task.

A thorough demographic analysis might take from several weeks to several months and may require outside help if the congregation is large. Organizations stand ready to help define an audience so preaching can meet their needs more effectively.[1]

That may sound daunting, but don't get discouraged. You don't need to know all there is to know to preach a relevant sermon. Without taking the time and money for a full–scale analysis, sermon applications can be sharpened by a basic knowledge of the people and community. Start by dividing the congregation into a few simple categories (men, women, children) and subcategories (such as working mothers, single parents, and teenagers). Consult this list from week to week to make sure you are speaking to

1. Aubrey Malphurs, *Planting Growing Churches for the Twenty–first Century* (Grand Rapids: Baker, 1992), 165–68.

all the groups in your church. You can be as detailed as you want with these subcategories (occupation, hobbies), but don't overanalyze. A few categories probably will suffice, especially in a smaller church.

Of course, you gain two strokes if you grew up in the community in which you pastor. While there are disadvantages to being a prophet in your home town, there are also some decided advantages. The best thing is that less time is needed to find the pulse of the community. The pastor can celebrate reunions rather than building all new bridges into people's lives. The pastor who occupies the post of friend, confidant, and neighbor can sculpt applications to fit needs precisely.

Find a purpose

However the needs in a congregation come to light, the preacher aware of them is free to develop messages with a particular purpose in mind. At this point in sermon preparation we need to determine that *homiletical purpose.*[2]

Returning to the analogy of archery, the preacher stands poised, aiming an arrow at a target with a large red bull's eye. The arrow is the sermon, and the bull's eye is the purpose of your sermon. In archery, as in preaching, the target should be clearly defined, sharply drawn. The careful archer keeps his eyes glued to the target . . . focused . . . undistracted by other potential targets.

With purpose defined carefully, the target almost attracts the arrow as a super magnet would draw iron. The purpose effectively draws the sermon to itself. As an arrow in flight, the message will not wander; it will stay on course

2. We will distinguish between purpose and goal as follows: *Purpose* will refer to that which the communicator desires to accomplish in the lives of the audience through communication. *Goals* will refer to the specific steps to be taken to achieve that purpose.

until it strikes home. Carefully define purpose, and chances are good that you will hit the bull's eye.

Let's change the analogy. In preaching, when you express your purpose carefully, the sermon leaps to embrace the application with the natural attraction of Romeo to Juliet. Nothing could keep those two apart. When you think of application you may think first of appealing to the will, telling people what to do and how to do it. But the will is only truly engaged if the heart and mind join hands. Aim first for the heart. Then, when you tell them what to do, people will understand how to fulfil the desire of their heart. You will release them to joyful obedience rather than burdening them with obligations.

Forming a homiletical purpose also has the practical aspect of efficiency: it will help keep a sermon on track; you find yourself eliminating superfluous illustrations and unnecessary details.

A sermon becomes more sharply defined overall as this excess is stripped away. In exegesis you entered a forest of biblical possibilities and felled a single tree. In the theological step you planed the tree down to a log, but it's hard to launch a log from a bowstring with much force. In the homiletical step you whittle the theological log down to a sharply–pointed arrow with a target in mind.

The purpose statement at the homiletical step is a bit different from the purpose statements for either the exegetical or the theological stages. In those stages we considered the purpose of the author in relating to the original audience (exegetical), and the purpose of the Holy Spirit in communicating timeless principles to all people in all times (theological). In the homiletical stage we concentrate on change in *our* audience.

What is this text calling this people to believe, feel, or do? Try formulating the purpose statement something like this:

> I believe the text is calling on us to *believe more strongly* that. . . .
>
> I believe the text is calling on us to *feel more deeply* that. . . .
>
> I believe the text is calling on us to *do more readily* (the following). . . .

To believe, to feel, or to do; these three actions address the whole man or woman. *To believe* addresses the intellect, *to feel* pricks the emotions, and *to do* challenges the will. By formulating a precise purpose statement, we reach out to the whole person. We avoid the "Oz syndrome"— emotional "scarecrow" sermons that lack a brain, or intellectual "tin woodsman" sermons that need a heart.

Of course, the "wonderful wizard" had only to point out that beating beneath the tinny exterior of the woodsman was the tender heart he always longed for, and the scarecrow had much more than straw for brains. Many of the tinny sermons we have heard are born of a tender heart; many sensationalistic sermons spring from keen minds. God has given us all the tools we need to preach a balanced message—a finely-honed purpose will encourage you to find that balance.

While we may include more than one purpose in a sermon (people may need to *think* and *feel* before they will *act*), each sermon should have a single dominant purpose. This overarching purpose will suggest a structure and emphasis and help govern the selection of details and supporting materials.

The sermon on Matthew 15:1–28 has an overarching purpose that focuses on action. It might be:

> To encourage seminarians to take time to worship Jesus in the quiet of their own hearts this Christmas.

If I want them to actually *do* this I must convince them from the text that this is what God wants and then motivate them sufficiently to act on their conviction. That's going to take an appeal to the mind *and* the heart.

Motivate toward the purpose

As we contemplate a purpose that will touch mind and heart we need to remember that every sermon should include one, and sometimes both, of two motivational elements: jeopardy and reward. The emotion most closely allied to jeopardy is fear—fear of loss. The emotion tied to reward is desire. It is a fact that those who hear and understand God's Word stand to lose something (jeopardy) if they fail to act on this new knowledge; they also stand to gain something if they act in faith, believing in God and that he is a rewarder of those who diligently seek him.

In using jeopardy and reward as motivations for obedience, our purpose is not to manipulate, but to reveal the reasonableness, the desirability of obedience to God's Word. We imitate what Jesus did in his own preaching and teaching. We may tend to think of Jesus as the gentle Shepherd who cared for the children in Matthew 18. He is, however, also the Lion of the tribe of Judah who could roar out judgment on hypocritical self–righteousness. You can practically smell the sulfur and feel the scorching heat in the parable of the rich man and Lazarus (Luke 16). Jesus never hesitated to underscore the jeopardy, the danger of desperate loss, which was the inevitable result of rejecting him. In fact, he spoke more about hell and its torment than anyone else in the Bible.

As preachers of God's Word we need to remind ourselves and our people that the greatest reward is heaven and fellowship with God, and the most severe loss is hell and separation from God. As we walk our daily paths we consistently take steps in one of those two directions. It is our duty as emissaries of God to reveal and cajole, but not to coerce movement in a heavenly direction. The steps we encourage them to take may be small and seemingly insignificant; however, we must stress that there are rewards to gain, joys to experience and painful losses to sustain all along the way. It all depends on which path they decide to take. In each message our purpose is to transport our people to a place where they can make wise decisions to move in a heavenly direction based on a clear understanding of God's Word.

We may need to convince them of the benefits of treating one's wife with the dignity of a delicate vase instead of like a cast-iron washtub. We may need to explain how teenagers can honor parents by obeying them. We may need to show them how to slice through steel apron strings and follow Christ into some vocational ministry.

Wrapped in each message—in its structure, its emphasis, its illustrations, and its applications—is an appeal to desire and/or fear. This appeal may, but does not always, involve desire of heaven and/or fear of hell. All the elements of the message will anticipate objections or questions or obstacles to appropriate action. Explain, convince, and apply as needed throughout and as time allows.

Overcome obstacles to application

Now it's time to ask three *focusing questions* individuals before you may be asking.[3] Each of the questions uncovers obstacles lying in the path of effective communication of God's Word. Answering these questions will influence both structure and emphasis in the homiletical outline. The three questions are:

1. What does it mean?
2. Is it really true?
3. So what difference does it make?

3. Haddon W. Robinson calls these the "developmental questions." *Biblical Preaching* (Grand Rapids: Baker, 1980), 81–99.

I don't understand. Please explain.

To remember the three questions, think of the Israelites' experience with the manna in the wilderness. They walk out early one morning to see the desert floor layered with something white and bread like. The first words out of their mouths were the same *we* say when we come upon something new and different: "What is it?"[4]

That's the first question you need to ask regarding your audience: What needs to be explained? Are theological terms lying about in the message that have never been explained to these people in a clear and memorable way? Explain when explaining is necessary. People have to know what you are talking about before they can apply it.

How many in your congregation could give a concise, accurate definition of sanctification or justification? Too often we pepper our people with theological buckshot—and rack up predictable results. They get stung and before long they learn to duck when they see another verbal barrage on the way. If we are to throw something, let's be a quarterback who throws a touchdown pass rather than a hunter firing off a painful bullet.

In addition to explaining theological terms, a preacher often must unravel the biblical context, for example, the relationship between Jews and Samaritans that shows the significance of Jesus' stop at the well in Samaria and his words with a Samaritan woman. Explaining the term or the relationship or the setting in vivid language does more than inform—it helps the audience crystallize the thought. Once you create for them a vivid impression of the meaning of God's Word, you automatically invite them to participate in a true learning experience.

---

4. The Hebrew word, *manna* may be translated, "what is it?"

Prove it, and I'll believe it.

Now, back to the desert with the Israelites for our second question. Again, you are an Israelite standing just outside your tent. You see the white substance on the ground and ask, "Manna—What is it?" Moses says, "Why, it's bread from heaven!" But you have never seen bread from heaven—nothing like this has ever happened before, and you are a bit skeptical. So, you ask, "How do I know what you say is true? Prove it to me." The congregation may understand what is said, but they may not buy it.

In preaching from Ephesians 5 on the respective roles of husband and wife a preacher can anticipate with some confidence that the minute the word *submit* is uttered the hair on some necks will start bristling. You may do a whale of a job explaining what biblical submission means (for husbands as well as for wives), but the clearer you make it, the more you sense the natives growing restless.

Preaching from some passages is like handling a live grenade. It's as if God pulled the pin and handed you the grenade—all you can do is toss it out to the congregation and dive for cover! These explosive texts require great care and sensitivity to prevailing cultural biases if we are to persuade people to obey God's Word. We do not water down the truth, but in giving truth we approach those who may be offended with tact and respect for long-held, and sometimes tightly-clinched, opinions. The truth will detonate, but we want it to knock down defenses, not blow up bridges that took years to build.

So what do I do about it?

If our purpose is transformation rather than mere information we want God's people to be changed rather than merely challenged, so we build bridges instead of barricades. A well–made bridge will connect people to God's Word and to other people. Building bridges takes a commitment to practical application. To learn how to do that, let's go back to the wilderness.

You have seen the manna. You know what it is and you are convinced that it is truly a miraculous supply of bread from the hand of God himself. Now, the third question is the most obvious, and perhaps because it is so obvious it is the most neglected of the three. The question is, "So what difference does it make?"

"OK, I understand what it is, and I believe it is as you say it is, but what am I supposed to do now with this new knowledge?"

In the case of the manna, Moses' answer was simple: "Eat it." Applying God's Word to the lives of his people should be as natural and as self-evident as eating a meal placed in front of you. Too often our problem in delivering sermons is that we spend all of our time describing the food and forget to tell the people what to do with it.

While we never want to talk down to our congregation, we do need to realize that the majority are spiritual babes, and babies need to be shown what to do with food. With infants and toddlers food sometimes makes the appointed rendezvous, but most of it winds up on the wall or the floor or the head. Playing with food is great fun, but it doesn't get the job done. Both physical food and God's Word are designed to nourish—one the body, the other the soul. Neither will work unless they get deep inside where they can do some good. Helping people apply the Word and showing how to eat that which is "sweeter than honey" (Pss. 19:9–11; 119:103) creates in them a desire for more and shows them how to live God's way. This is the fulfillment of the preacher's task.

As you anticipate and overcome such obstacles to application your sermons will take on greater practical urgency, a sense of being "just right" for *this* congregation. There is no such thing as a generic sermon—one size fits all—because there is no such thing as a generic audience. Each congregation has its own unique needs; an effective sermon is a custom fit.

In doing the theological step (see chap. 2) the preacher will discover universal needs of all people of all times, real needs of men and women from God's perspective. Answering the homiletical focusing questions of *What does this mean? Is it really true?* and *So what difference does it make to me?* will help meet the *real needs* through the heart door of *felt needs*. By exploring and discovering answers to these questions you will be able to structure your sermons more effectively and emphasize those points that truly need development.

You need to ask all three questions of your central proposition as well as your outline. If, at any point, your congregation would ask one or more of the questions, that issue must be dealt with at that point in the message. You may need to address one or more of these questions several times through the sermon. In some cases people may not need much time spent on either of the first two—but they *always* need to be shown what to do and how to do it.

Write a homiletical proposition

Once you have formulated the homiletical purpose and know the relevant application for the message you have discovered, try stating these as a *homiletical proposition.* The sermon on Matthew 15:1–28 was preached during a Christmas season in the chapel at Dallas Theological Seminary. The audience consisted of seminary students, professors, and staff. The focusing questions were asked with that audience in mind. Since it is easy in an academic environment to become academic in worship, the message aimed to recall the organic, devotional heart of our service. My homiletical proposition for Matthew 15:1–28 is, "Get right with Jesus—Go state of the heart."

Let's compare the three central propositions.

Exegetical central proposition: Jesus teaches the Jewish
Pharisees and a Gentile woman that they cannot establish a right relationship with God by keeping religious
rules; they must respond to Christ in faith.

Theological central proposition: People obtain a right relationship with God by recognizing personal insufficiency
and by placing faith in God's sufficiency.

Homiletical central proposition: Get right with Jesus—Go
state of the heart.

The homiletical proposition is shorter than the other
two. It employs only one two-syllable word (Jesus), and it
puts a twist on the stock phrase, "state of the art." Perhaps
most important for application, it is a command, rather
than a simple declarative sentence as in the exegetical and
theological central propositions. The nature of the command is still a puzzle: what does it mean to "go state of the
heart"? Hopefully, by the end of the sermon, everyone will
understand what it means and will want to do it. The homiletical proposition doesn't have to explain or list everything that needs doing. That would be rather pedantic and
less than memorable. The homiletical proposition simply
needs to challenge the status quo accurately and memora-
bly and with a view to positive change.

The first stage is now complete. In part 1 you have col-
lected and refined your biblical fuel. You have done the
hard work of digging out the exegetical information. You
have refined that data in a timeless theological outline, and
you have asked the developmental questions. In part 2 we
will discover how to custom–design your sermon so that it
will carry your congregation to a region of personal discovery and challenge.

Chapter summary:

Proposition, purpose, and destination

1. Analyze the audience.
2. Develop a purpose statement with those people in mind.
3. Ask the three focusing questions about this audience: (1) What does it mean? (2) Is it really true? (3) So what difference does it make?
4. Write a the homiletical proposition based on the answers to those questions.

Part 2
Building the Rocket

4

Installing the Ignition System: Introductions

How Do I Get Started?

T minus eight.

In the first structural step the emphases are on clarity and interest.

In chapter 3 we arrived at a homiletical goal and a homiletical proposition. My goal for this sermon, with a seminary congregation in mind, was "to encourage seminarians to take time to worship Jesus in the quiet of their own hearts this Christmas." For the homiletical proposition, we suggested, "Get right with Jesus—Go state of the heart." Now we focus on how to structure the message to arrive at the goal of specific life change.

Think of the sermon as having three stages, like the three stages of a rocket. The first stage is the introduction, the second stage is the body, and the third stage is the conclusion. Every sermon you ever preach will have these three large parts. Graphically these parts may be viewed as

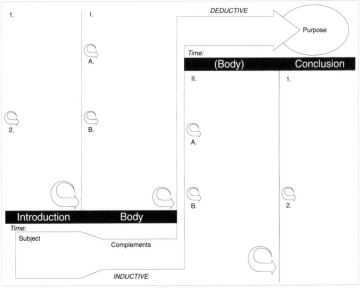

Figure 4.1

a model—the power sermon model, which is illustrated in Figure 4.1.[1]

Let's take a close look at the first stage: the introduction. Introductions serve five basic purposes:

1. to create interest;
2. to reveal need;
3. to orient the audience to the subject;
4. to orient the audience to the biblical text, and
5. to give the audience a structural overview of the sermon.

Create interest

Why bother raising interest? Doesn't that take time away from the exposition of the Word? Not really. Taking

1. The model used for this sermon is the inductive-deductive form. It would be helpful for the reader to review Appendix B to see the deductive and inductive models. A discussion of the models is found on pages 176–85.

time to create interest is like taking time to plow the field before you plant the seed. Hard, untilled hearts are out there. If you take the time to sow the Word, you owe it to yourself and to your hearers to make sure the soil is ready to receive it. Then get ready for a bumper crop of understanding. But taking time to create interest goes beyond the practical benefits of greater potential for comprehension. It is simply good form.

Even if we preach in the same church week after week we need to earn the right to be heard each time we enter the pulpit. How arrogant I am if I assume that just because I stand behind a pulpit people will automatically listen. Some preachers work like homiletical John Waynes. They mount the pulpit and ride herd over a bunch of spiritual tenderfeet: "Listen up, pilgrims," they shout, "you joined on for tough times, and I'm the man to show 'em to ya!" The time has come to start earning the right to be heard each time we speak.

We earn that right, personally and professionally. Personal integrity demands that we make sure our walk matches our talk. We must live in the power of the Holy Spirit. That allows us to enter the pulpit in his strength rather than running on compressed hot air.

These are tough times for preachers, especially those in high profile ministries. Never before has the public eye been so probing. Never before has fault been so easy to find. Life in the fishbowl can become life in the toilet bowl for Christian leaders who are not careful to "walk in a manner worthy of the calling with which you have been called" (Eph. 4:1 NASB; see also Col. 1:10).

We also earn the right to be heard through professional integrity to speak with authority on the Bible and how it applies. The professional pays the price for the incredible privilege of explaining God's Word. The people must know that their preacher knows the Bible. If you have done the work in chapters 1 through 3, you should have no problem here. Knowledge of the Bible is important, but it is at least as important that your flock be convinced that you know and love them. A congregation's love for their pastor will cover a multitude of homiletical sins.

One way to show a concern for listeners is to grace pulpit communication with a good introduction. Such an introduction meets listeners on common ground, talking about shared interests. It's a simple courtesy, but it reminds people that this sermon is plugged into their reality. Starting from a point of shared interest takes preaching out of the ivory tower and plants its message firmly on the asphalt of everyday life. It illustrates graphically that you can live joyfully in the world without getting snagged on the world's unwholesome values. The preacher begins by tying the message to some aspect of the congregation's interests and concerns. The sermon becomes identified with the broad range of life interests.

Of course, the interests touched on relate directly to the message. For a sermon on 1 Corinthians 13, the great love chapter, you might begin with a stanza from a love ballad that would be recognizable to the audience. When you recite (or sing if you are truly brave—and have a good voice) the words to a well-known song a number of people will silently mouth the words along with you. Songs or the words to songs evoke memories of people and places that are often so poignant they can rekindle an old "love feeling" or open old wounds.

This is where knowing a congregation becomes critical. Cole Porter won't fly at a college retreat, nor Hammer in a retirement center. Find the music, the poetry, the story, or the illustration that *fits* the group. If you find yourself saying, "Yeah, they'll relate to that," the introduction probably is a winner. An introduction builds from what interests *others*—not always what *you* want to talk about.

We will say more about illustrations in chapter 9. For now we note that the world is full of them. We just need to learn to spot them. They can come from television shows, books, nature, our own experiences, and sports. Try going somewhere—anywhere—*without* finding an illustration. Finding just the *right* illustration may be a different story. For the introduction seek a story or quote that rivets attention on the subject. Think of this first brief story as the wide mouth of a funnel: It starts broadly but quickly narrows the focus. Such a story says, "The (issue, problem, puzzle, challenge, question, pain, celebration, warning, disaster) we face today is the same as the world faces. Let's take a look at that problem and how the world handles it."

Never preach on a Sunday morning without first looking at the front page of the newspaper. Sure it's the last minute, but you need to be aware of late-breaking events. Several years ago one of the authors almost went to church to preach without following this rule. At the last minute he glanced at the paper and its huge banner headline: "DELTA CRASHES AT DFW!"[2] The car radio filled in some details on the way to church. News of the crash was on every band. Scores of people had died. The congregation was in shock.

Without referring to that tragedy the preacher would have revealed that he was pitifully ignorant of the world around him, or—worse—that he was callously indifferent. So the story of the crash became part of the sermon introduction. The field was ready to receive the Word; the Lord had plowed it. People were distracted, upset, looking for some assurance that God hadn't slipped up. It is the preacher's responsibility to be sensitive to the immediate, sometimes tragic, point of interest and use it as an entry point to get God's Word of comfort across. Be sensitive to events that are shaping the world, the country, and the community; build them into the introduction. Flexibility is

2. *DFW* is headlinese for the Dallas-Fort Worth International Airport.

an important lesson to learn in delivering an introduction that conveys the zip of spontaneity and the tranquillity of design.

In the Matthew 15 sermon, preached just before the Christmas holidays, the point of interest was the festive mood of the chapel crowd. All looked forward to getting out of classes and into some serious holiday fun. I found a quote in *Reader's Digest* I thought would work for an opening interest–grabber. I boiled it down to one sentence that would express not only the content but how it would work for me in the introduction. The first point on the outline of the introduction looked like this:

> Introduction
> 1. Becoming Santa Clause for my kids illustrates the fate of most dads who want to give the best to their families at Christmas.

Of course, it doesn't always work that way. Often we won't have just the right illustration, so we will jot down a note in our homiletical outline that will tell us what kind of opening material we need to create interest in our subject. It would look something like this:

> Introduction
> 1. Find an illustration or quote that will appeal to interest in Christmas and reveal our tendency to get swept up in materialism.

For the remainder of this outline we will assume we have found the material we will need to sketch the outline.

Now, go to the model (Fig. 4.2). The first point of the introduction should be written into the left column under *Introduction*.

Reveal a need

Once you have engaged the congregation's interest, bridge into an area of personal need. On the chart we will construct through the rest of this book are several curved arrows. Each indicates a transition. For example, notice an

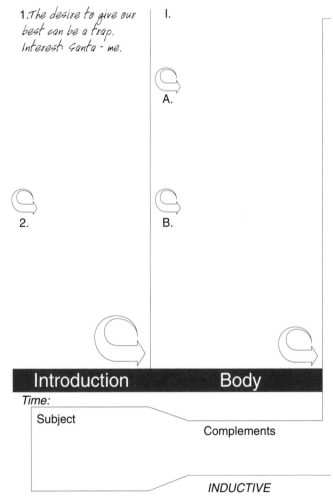

Figure 4.2

arrow below the Arabic numeral *1* in the Introduction. This arrow reminds of the importance of linking ideas so that one point flows naturally into the next.

The old dictum: "*A* must imply *B*; *B* must imply *C*" is still true. We cannot afford to assume that the audience makes the connection. They must have a good reason to move from *A* to *B*. Good transitions provide that reasonable link and show the progress of thought as the points unfold. For more on transitions, see chapter 5.

As the funnel narrows, the sharpening focus points to a problem that must be solved, a knot that needs untying. You must show why life has become all snarled and tangled and how God's Word untangles it. Often an audience enters the sanctuary oblivious to the need the sermon will address. It isn't that they don't have the need; they just aren't conscious of it at the moment. They know they need to feast on the Word, but they may have forgotten how satisfying it can be. The job of a communicator is to show people how hungry they really are—not for food that perishes, but for the Bread of life.

As a rule people prefer not to be reminded that they should eat well. They don't mind being reminded that they are hungry, as long as the reminder accompanies the opportunity to satisfy that hunger now. The spiritually starved, in particular, would rather remain comfortably ignorant of their need for solid food. The trend is for churchgoers to slowly embalm their souls on a diet of sugary platitudes and pseudo–spiritual junk food. Many prefer to starve to death spiritually rather than be reminded that they need a healthy diet of the Word. Such people want Shangri-la, and take great pains to find preachers who promise a shortcut into the mountains. Plenty of preachers willingly keep them fat and complacent, feeding congregations what they want rather than what they need.

There is nothing wrong in wanting heaven. All people long for the ideal life in which all problems are solved and joy overflows.[3] It's our privilege as messengers of the King to share the good news and so awaken in hearts a longing for Christ and his perfect kingdom. The problem isn't in longing for the ideal. The problem is in wanting a shortcut.

We in the congregation pretend, deny, lie to ourselves, rationalize our sin—anything to keep from looking in the mirror so that we must acknowledge that we are far too weak to make heaven, or as Christians to live victoriously, under our own steam. Why do we hide? It could be that we have insulated ourselves from that particular need simply because it is too unpleasant to face.

Anyone who has broken a leg knows a "special friend," one with a twisted sense of humor.

"You know what I hate?" they begin. "I hate it when you get that little itch right behind your knee and you want to scratch it so badly, but there's no way to get at it because of that dumb cast!"

Everything was fine. There wasn't an itch anywhere. But they made you think about it. Now you would do anything to get inside that cast for a little scratch.

Many folks sit before us with a cast around a broken heart. It may have been a rejection suffered years ago. Or they may have merely scuffed their pride in the parking lot on the way to church. The older injuries are hardest to get at. They have been plastered over with excuses and bitterness until the heart is covered with a protective cast of armor plate that is virtually impregnable. Nothing can penetrate our defense mechanisms—not sermons, not prayers, not friends. Unbelief and a hardened heart are the

3. C. S. Lewis explores our universal longing for joy in *Surprised by Joy: The Shape of My Early Life* (New York: Harcourt, Brace, 1956). Leland Ryken draws on the work of noted literary critic Northrop Frye to suggest a common structural pattern in world literature. The pattern incorporates the ideal society as that for which all people strive, and in which all joy resides. Leland Ryken, *The Literature of the Bible* (Grand Rapids: Zondervan, 1974), 14–25.

clamp and key that non-Christians construct to keep God locked out.

Even Christians build incredible walls to shut pain out, but of course all we really do is lock it in. We whisper to ourselves, "Time will take care of this." But bitter experience teaches that time doesn't heal all wounds—it just anesthetizes them. The pain may hibernate, but it's still alive down deep inside. Most of us live in a secret fear of its waking.

Our job as preachers isn't to crack the cast or to rouse and slay the sleeping dragon. Those who try only appear too threatening or too clumsy. People run from preachers who approach with a hammer and saw. It is the preacher's calling to remind hearers of the itch and so to nudge individuals gently to look again at their need. We are to create in them a desire to let God remove the cast and heal their wounded heart.

Remember that our model sermon was designed for a seminary audience, but the needs of seminarians aren't very different from those of the rest of the world—they just manifest themselves in ways unique to an academic environment. Students and faculty alike are *interested* in Christmas for all the traditional reasons . . . *plus* one: the opportunity to minister. Christmas season can be one of the busiest times of the year for seminarians. There's a special thrill in pointing people to the Son of God lying in a manger. It's one of the many privileges of being in vocational ministry.

But the shared interest can lead to a shared need—the need to spend less time ministering and more time worshiping. Ministries are good in themselves, but it is easy to allow them to become a substitute for a relationship with the Lord. In short, those of us with busy ministry schedules can easily begin to worship the service of our Lord rather than the Lord of our service.

The danger is all the more unnerving for its charm and subtlety. The good so often seduces us. It's a brilliant strategy on Satan's part: Make us fall in love with "the ministry," and soon we forget the One we serve. Allow us even moderate success and we will become so enchanted with our own Pharisaical practice that we wouldn't even recognize the Lord if he walked into our midst.

Encourage someone to settle for *doing* (the work of the ministry) rather than *being* (a Christian through whom Christ lives) and before long you will have a plastic imitation servant. This robot looks good on the outside, but he or she is just going through the motions without any heart. The person has seen enough of the real thing to generate some pretty convincing fruit of the spirit. But it is plastic; it may look good on camera, but it will not provide any nourishment.

Plastic ministers all begin with a desire to serve. They are equipped to minister. "Now," they think, "I'm ready. I'm strong. Satan may get me somewhere else, but he'll never get me here!" Of course that's right where the attack comes—where we perceive ourselves to be strongest and best equipped. Satan knows where we are most confident we are most vulnerable. And that vulnerability doesn't just apply to seminarians.

Therefore, the *need* point of the introduction outline for Matthew 15 looks like this:

Introduction
1. Interest: we all want to enhance our relationships with our families and with the Lord by giving them our best, especially at Christmas.
2. Need: the desire to give our best can subtly trap us into substituting ministry for relationship.

On the model we can synthesize the second point under the *Introduction* and write it in to the space provided under the far-left column (Fig. 4.3).

Orient to the subject

At some point in the introduction we must address the subject of the sermon. When a story, a quote, or an illustra-

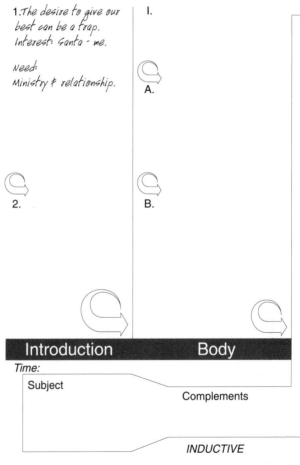

Figure 4.3

tion creates interest, the interest created must be directed toward the subject. Reveal too how the congregation's need relates to the subject. Remember that the introduction is a funneling process. Begin broadly, but narrow your focus quickly to a poignant consideration of the subject at hand. Through an interesting and need-arousing introduction the audience realizes the importance of considering the subject:

> Why we should take time to worship Jesus this Christmas . . .
> Whom we should treat with respect . . .
> How we respond when we are mistreated . . .
> When it is OK to be angry with God . . .
> Where we should start trying to reach the world with the gospel . . .
> What the essence is of the true gospel of Jesus Christ . . .

Use interest and need to orient your congregation to your subject.

Orient to the text

Now that you have raised interest, addressed need, and oriented listeners to the subject, build a bridge back to the world of the Bible, specifically to the passage to be exposited.

This is no small task. While most Christians esteem the Bible highly, for many it remains a remote and mysterious collection of stories and rules. For some the message has been drummed in since childhood that they aren't smart enough to figure out the Bible on their own. Besides, who would want to bother? For many, reading the Bible is way too close to their high school history class. It seems boring and irrelevant. "Let the preacher or teacher tell me what it means. At least he throws in a joke every now and then."

The secret to making the Bible come alive is two-fold. First, find parallels between the biblical situation and the contemporary world. Second, read the passage well.[4]

Finding parallels between our situation and the biblical story is like tracing threads in a garment. The more connecting threads we find, the stronger the identification. The stronger those connections with the ancient world, the more likely people will want to emulate or avoid the biblical example. Connections reveal that the problems we face are not that different from those faced by Moses or Saul or Peter. Moses struggled with impatience; so do we. Saul was vain; so are we. Peter was impetuous; so are we.

But we share more than problems with the men and women of the Bible. We share the same problem-solving God. The lessons God taught them are for our benefit, our instruction. Establish the parallels in the introduction, then continually reinforce and build on them throughout the sermon. It is like weaving a garment. By the end of the message, a strong, thick fabric of thought has been created, a practical message that can be taken out and applied against harsh realities of life. It all starts in the introduction.

Take time to paint the scene with words. Help the audience see the tabernacle and hear the bleating of the sheep. Let them smell and taste the sacrifice. Allow them to feel the sand under their feet as they enter the courtyard. The more detail you add to the biblical setting, the more they will immerse their imagination in that world. As you read, take time to see the images. If you "see it" in your imagination, chances are that the audience will "see it" too. If you don't, most of them never will. The basic rule is, "Think it before you say it." Really think about what you are reading. You are speaking *thoughts*, not just *words* on a page.

---

4. For a detailed explanation of the reading process, see Reg Grant and John Reed, *Telling Stories to Touch the Heart* (Wheaton, Ill.: Victor, 1990), 37–52.

Speak them to an audience as if they are hearing them for the first time.

Setting the scene in this way can have some stunning effect. People begin to see the Bible, not as a dusty book that must be explained by another, but as a wonderful map that leads them across uncharted seas to an unexplored land. The Bible will come alive for them. Bible characters will emerge as true individuals. They will begin to replace the crayon colored figures of their childhood with three-dimensional, multifaceted personalities. Here, in the world you recreate, many will discover for the first time a David of flesh and blood instead of Renaissance marble.

As you work your way through the Bible, your congregation will grow to appreciate subtle differences among characters—the rich texturing and shadings in a gallery of authentic humanity at its best and worst. They will find people in the Bible to be amazingly like themselves. And if that happens, who knows? We may actually encourage them to pick up the Scriptures and read for themselves! They may see the consequences of sin clearly for the first time and decide to turn to Christ for help. They may even see the joy that is set before them and decide to take up the cross, to pay the price of discipleship, and follow the Savior.

For Matthew 15, the third point of the introduction looks like this:

Introduction
1. Interest: We all want to enhance our relationships with our families and with the Lord by giving them our best, especially at Christmas.
2. Need: The desire to give our best can subtly trap us into substituting ministry for relationship.
3. Orientation to subject: We need to be careful to maintain a right relationship with Jesus this Christmas.

4. Orientation to text: The Pharisees substituted ministry for relationship when they relied on their "state of the art" training to qualify them before the Lord.

Give a structural overview

Now take just a sentence to show where you are going structurally. Let hearers know that you will be "considering," "looking at," "discovering" the answer to a problem you share with the biblical audience. That answer (or answers) is your complement. Be specific:

This morning Paul is going to reveal *three ways* to fight sexual temptation.

Today we will discover from the life of David the *one thing* you need to do to get right with God when you have blown it big time.

This evening we will find out from James *three actions* we can take to control our tongue.

The fifth point in the introduction for Matthew 15 looks like this:

Introduction
1. Interest: We all want to enhance our relationships with our families and with the Lord by giving them our best, especially at Christmas.
2. Need: The desire to give our best can subtly trap us into substituting ministry for relationship.
3. Orientation to subject: We need to be careful to maintain a right relationship with Jesus this Christmas.
4. Orientation to text: The Pharisees substituted ministry for relationship when they relied on their "state of the art" training to qualify them before the Lord.

5. Structural Overview: This morning we will consider one way to maintain a right relationship with Jesus this Christmas.

Now boil down these last two points of the introduction and place them in the left column of the model (Fig. 4.4). At this point you may wish to read the text for the morn-

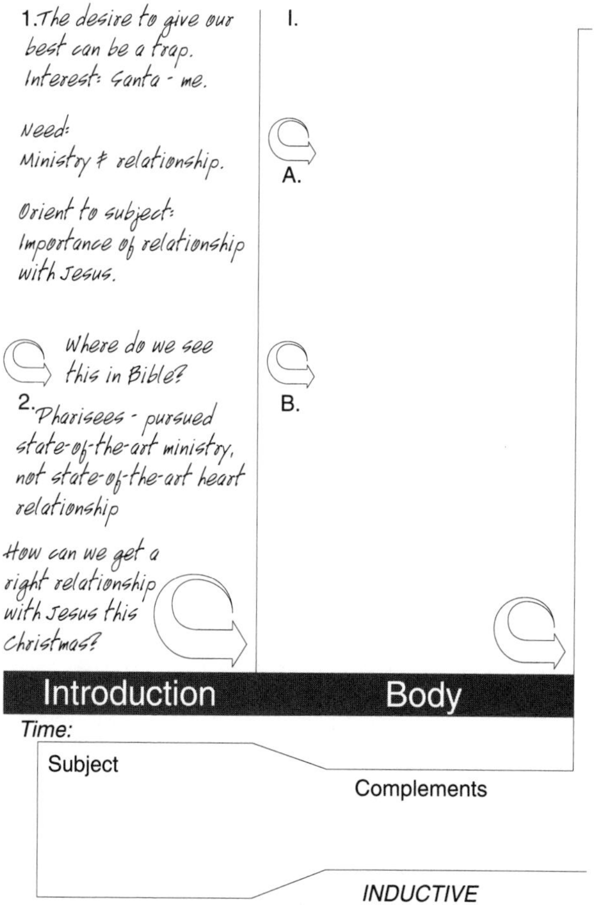

1. The desire to give our best can be a trap. Interest: Santa - me.

Need: Ministry & relationship.

Orient to subject: Importance of relationship with Jesus.

Where do we see this in Bible?

2. Pharisees - pursued state-of-the-art ministry, not state-of-the-art heart relationship

How can we get a right relationship with Jesus this Christmas?

I.

A.

B.

Introduction   **Body**

Time:

Subject

Complements

INDUCTIVE

Figure 4.4

ing. There is no fixed rule about where to read Scripture. Different occasions call for reading at different places in the order of worship. Nor do you need to feel obligated to read all the text at once. You may wish to read only that part of the text that you will cover under the first main point of the outline. Whatever you decide, indicate the place of the reading in your outline and on the model.

The first stage of the rocket is complete. By the end of the introduction your people should be saying to themselves, "I'm *interested*, and I *need* this message." They should be interested not only in where you want to take them—They should realize they *need* to go there.

In chapter 5 we will concentrate on constructing the body of a message that will carry them to that destination.

Chapter summary:

Introductions

1. Introduce the audience to your subject through an interesting illustration or quote.
2. Remind the audience of their need.
3. Use interest and need to orient listeners to the subject.
4. Acquaint them with the text, drawing parallels between the Bible's world and ours.
5. Give a structural preview of where you are taking them.

5

Creating the Navigational System: Body and Transitions

How Do I Keep from Missing a Turn on the Way to My Destination?

T minus seven.

In the second structural step we aim at clarity.

You have just finished the first stage of the sermon, the introduction. At this point the congregation is interested in where you are going, primarily because they now sense that they will be better off for having made the trip. You have raised a question, revealed a problem, created an itch—and denied them an easy way out. No more excuses. No more rationalizing their sin. You have brought them face to face with an undeniable need. Tension exists, and it can't be ignored. Now you must show them what God's Word has to say about it.

In this second stage of the message it is your privilege as well as your obligation to do three things:

1. You must help people understand what the Lord has to say about their need and how to solve it.
2. They must be convinced that God's solution is preferable to any alternative.
3. You must show them how to apply what they understand and are convinced of.

The body and transitions function as a navigational system to keep the sermon on course, focused on those points that progress toward the intended destination.

Transitions

After you have read the text, supply a brief transitional statement to the first main point.

From James 3—
"If you really want to stop the gossip that's tearing this church apart we can get started this morning!"

From 2 Corinthians 5—
"Before we can understand why sanctification is so important we have to understand what sanctification means."

From Exodus 18—
"Let me paint for you a portrait of a frustrated leader."

From Ephesians 5—
"Why does the Lord place such a high value on a wife submitting to her husband?"

From Revelation 21—
"Did you ever wonder what heaven will be like?"

From Proverbs 31—
"Let's take a look at a world-class home maker."

From Proverbs 5—
"Let's take a look at a world-class home breaker."

A good transition welds one piece of the sermon to the next. The better the weld, the tighter the connection. The tighter the connection between the parts of the sermon, the easier it will be for a congregation to see the whole. The parts will appear to fit together perfectly like well-cut stones, needing no cement. A good transition does not draw attention to itself. It flows unobtrusively into the next point. According to John Broadus, "the transitions from one part of a discourse to the next are most felicitous when least noticeable."[1] An effective transition works almost magically to quietly produce the next point. A good transition is the set-up line to the punch line.

A transition by itself is incomplete. Remember that what comes first sets up, and makes the listener want, what comes next. The introduction sets up the reading of the text, which in turn sets up the first main point.

On the model jot down the transition line in the second column, just before the first main point.

Body

The form of the first main point will depend on the overall development of the message. Development of the message will depend on the answers to the focusing questions. If some theological terms should be explained (focusing question one), a definition of key terms should come early on. If you need to convince people of your interpretation of the text (focusing question two), the sermon should be structured as an argument. If this audience will understand and have no problem accepting the message, the primary focus can be on application (focusing question three).

It is important when deciding how best to structure the sermon to correctly anticipate the questions that may arise

1. John Broadus, *On the Preparation and Delivery of Sermons* (New York: Harper and Row, 1944), 119.

in the minds of people in the congregation. We often find that the *apparent* answer to the focusing questions is not always the *real* answer. For example, when we deliver a message on "holiness" to a seminary audience we might think, "they already know what holiness means (after all, they *are* seminary students), and they certainly won't have any problem in accepting the biblical idea that we ought to be holy. So why don't we see more legitimate holiness around here? It must be they just don't know how."

So we construct a message on "Five Steps to Holiness." Everybody nods in the right places and takes a few notes (on illustrations for future reference). Then the seminarians leave chapel wondering why they can't ever seem to be as holy as they would like to be.

Probe for the "real" questions

The problem with this sermon on holiness is not that the preacher answered the wrong question. The problem is that the preacher assumed these people automatically understood (or remembered) what "holiness" means. Perhaps only a few of these seminarians would be able to spout a textbook definition, and some who could give a definition might not own a comprehensive understanding.

The preacher also assumed that seminarians really want to be holy. That might not be wholly true. The fact is, finding accurate answers to such questions can be a sticky problem, but the speaker needs to probe to go beyond typical surface applications.

This is particularly true in sermons on being holy or good or patient or having any fruit of the Spirit. The majority—whether seminarians or not—who say they want these virtues are like well-intentioned dreamers who say they want to be writers. Someone summed up the attitude of such wannabe writers, "Most don't want to write. They want to have written." They want the job to be done, the struggle to be over, and the check to be in the mail.

Preachers answering the focus questions for such a sermon must keep in mind that holiness, like good writing, doesn't come easily, and it doesn't come cheap. We may want others to *think of* us as holy. Or we may want to have already become holy and embrace the mistaken notion that holiness is something to arrive at and then coast through life. Worse, we may labor under the legalistic tendency to manufacture holiness through unceasing activity. But few want to lead the disciplined spiritual life—paradoxically, a life of dynamic yieldedness to the control of the Spirit—that leads to a consistently holy lifestyle.

Our job as communicators is to convince our listeners of the desirability of holiness. We must motivate them to pursue holiness at any cost. That is how the homiletical purpose should work. Whatever the homiletical purpose, be careful to anticipate the *real* roadblocks to application.

Build a skeleton

Once the real questions are pinned down, you are ready to structure the body of the sermon. Don't worry about writing out the sermon yet. All you want to do at this point is to construct the homiletical outline. Remember that the outline is merely the skeleton of the message. We will supply the flesh and blood when we prepare the manuscript. Still, the outline of the sermon is going to determine an approach to the truth to be conveyed.

Let's use the Matthew 15:1–28 sermon as an example.

In this sermon we don't reveal the homiletical central proposition until the second main point, but we can prepare the audience for that point by planting key words from the central proposition along the way. The central proposition is, "Get right with Jesus—Go state of the heart." In the introduction we used the key phrase "state of the art" to describe the external "equipment" of ministry and to help create a hook in the mind of the audience that will readily snag the homiletical proposition when it comes floating by.

Matthew 15:1–28 focuses on the contrast between the self-righteous Pharisees and an "unclean" Canaanite woman as they respond to Jesus. The story in Matthew flows from the negative (the Pharisees' arrogant response) to the positive (the woman's humble response) and so affords a great opportunity to close on an uplifting note. The first point covers Jesus' encounter with the Pharisees. It is stated with an implied warning for a contemporary audience:

> I. (Matt. 15:1–20) You aren't guaranteed a right relationship with God through state of the art externals.

Now, the anticipated question in the minds of the audience is, "What kind of externals is he talking about? At this point the background studies on the Pharisees become useful illustrative material. The goal here is to help the audience discover something they share with the Pharisees.

> A. You aren't guaranteed a right relationship with God through state of the art education.

Note the greater degree of specificity in the A level. The word *externals* was replaced with *education*. Now the preacher needs to develop that connection to the Pharisees.

> 1. The Pharisees had a state of the art education.
> 2. We have a state of the art education.

Note, we are not decrying the externals as evil in themselves. They were and are the gracious provision of the Lord. At this point we are simply making the observation that a shared advantage can lead to a shared arrogance. We began with the abstract idea of education; now we move to the more concrete image of the classrooms.

> B. You aren't guaranteed a right relationship with God in a state of the art facility.
>   1. The Pharisees had a state of the art facility.
>   2. We have a state of the art facility.

Next we move to the root of the problem. We share something with the Pharisees that we may not have really thought about. We share with them the true revelation of God in the Scriptures. With great privilege comes great responsibility, and the chance to abuse both.

> C. You aren't guaranteed a right relationship with God if you have a state of the art message.
>   1. The Pharisees had a state of the art message.
>   2. We have a state of the art message.

These parallels overcome our natural resistance to identifying with the Pharisees. By the end of the first main point the audience should clearly see that we share at least three advantages with the Pharisees that the Pharisees misused (See Fig. 5.1).

A transition to the next main point can summarize the warning of the first main point.

> Transition: We won't find a right relationship with God if we depend on state of the art to get us there.

Or the transition might review the development to that point and set up the next main point.

> Transition: If we can't get right with God using state of the art techniques, then how can we?

If the transition works as it should, the sermon will flow together seamlessly. The points will cease to be dry and didactic and will take on the naturally flowing character of the narrative itself. The negative lesson from the Pharisees can now be counterbalanced by a positive lesson in the next story. Again, look for the key word or phrase that will reinforce the lesson in the mind of the listener.

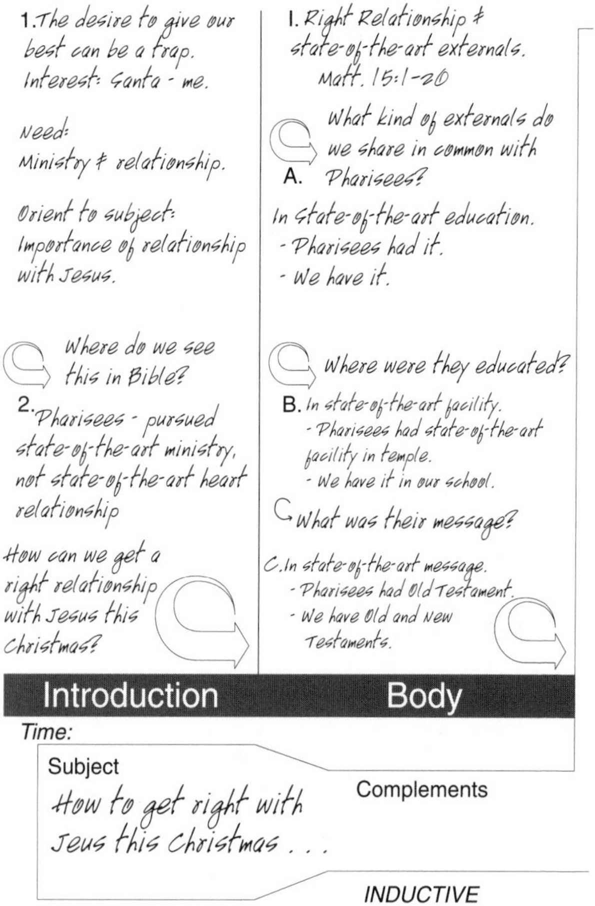

Figure 5.1

II. (Matt. 15:21–28) Get right with Jesus—Go state of the heart.

This point contrasts with the first point, using a word-play rhyme to aid memory. This is the homiletical proposition. Note again the command form. After hearing this point, the listener should be challenged to pause from preoccupation with the external tools of the ministry to consider the internal state of his or her heart.

Now it is time to return to the text to draw more connecting threads to the contrasting story of the Gentile woman. In the case of the Pharisees' encounter with Jesus we wanted to get the audience to recognize similarities with the Pharisees and so be warned. In the case of the Gentile woman, we want the audience to desire the qualities she exhibits and so be challenged.

A. (Matt. 15:21–24) The Gentile woman could appeal to no state of the art qualifications to recommend her to Jesus.

The woman lacked every advantage the Pharisees possessed. Now we will heighten the contrast between the Pharisees and the woman by examining the woman's position in that society. Again, the background studies on women in that part of the world reveal striking illustrative information.

1. (vv. 21–22). Her sex, her heritage, and her problem all worked against her.
   a. She was a woman and women were chattel.
   b. She was from Tyre and Sidon, the hometown of Jezebel and idolatrous worship.
   c. She had a demon-possessed daughter; children were lower than women on the social ladder.

The woman stands in direct contrast to the Pharisees; she enjoys neither social nor religious advantage. But there is usually a twist in the fabric of biblical characterization. Characters are rarely all bad or all good. They are simply human and so are realistically portrayed as a mix of good and bad. The woman had a wrong idea about Jesus as well. While the Pharisees rejected him because they wouldn't believe he could be the Jewish Messiah, the Gentile woman appealed to him because she believed him to be susceptible to flattery (she addresses him by his messianic title *Son of David*).

> 2. (vv. 23–24) Her manipulative appeal to Jesus as Jewish Messiah worked against her.

Jesus ignored her attempt to manipulate him with flattery. Now she casts aside all pretense and approaches him as we all should, with empty hands. Notice there is no direct application. The story moves quickly at this point, and a break for direct application would interrupt the flow and the force of the narrative.

> B. (Matt. 15:25–28) Her only hope was to appeal to Christ as her Lord.
> > 1. (vv. 25–27) Her appeal to Jesus as her Lord elicited his response.
> > > a. (v. 25) She acknowledged whom he was in bowing down to worship.
> > > b. (vv. 26–27) She acknowledged whom she was in her humble response to Jesus' observation.
> > 2. (v. 28) Jesus rewarded her humble faith.

Now we have completed the contrasting picture of the Gentile woman. Matthew presents her as the admirable one, even though she lacked any of the external qualifications for a right relationship with God. In the last point we will encourage a response like the woman's, then relate it to the seminary context. We open with a lesson from the text, then move quickly to a direct challenge.

> C. God readily extends his grace to anyone who bows before him with a humble heart.
> 1. A right relationship with God begins with a vision of who God really is.

The natural question at this point is, "What happens next?" Anticipate the question and the outline will flow naturally and seamlessly.

> 2. A vision of who God is will be followed by a humble acknowledgment of our need.
> 3. Once we sense our need of him we must take time out this busy Christmas season to be alone with the Lord.
> 4. Confess your desperate need of him with a humble heart.

This last point completes the body of the sermon. In a narrative sermon such as this there was little need for external illustration. The story of the two encounters with Jesus, enhanced with material from background studies, served the illustrative purpose of holding the interest of the audience while it taught the lesson.

Now summarize the content of your points and write them into your sermon chart. Don't worry about working in all the subpoints. Just indicate the main points and transitions. Pay particular attention to the transitions. You want to make sure the sermon unfolds naturally from point to point (see Fig. 5.2).

Create tension

A word of caution: We have been stressing logically necessary relationships between points. But the idea of building an airtight logical sequence may suggest that you should never create alternative scenarios, false paths, and tension. This is not the case. Use your subpoints on occasion to lead the audience down a dead-end street. Help them see that other ways they might turn lead nowhere.

For example, let's say the purpose of a sermon on 1 Thessalonians 5:6 is to encourage believers to be spiritually alert as they await the Lord's coming. Explore different

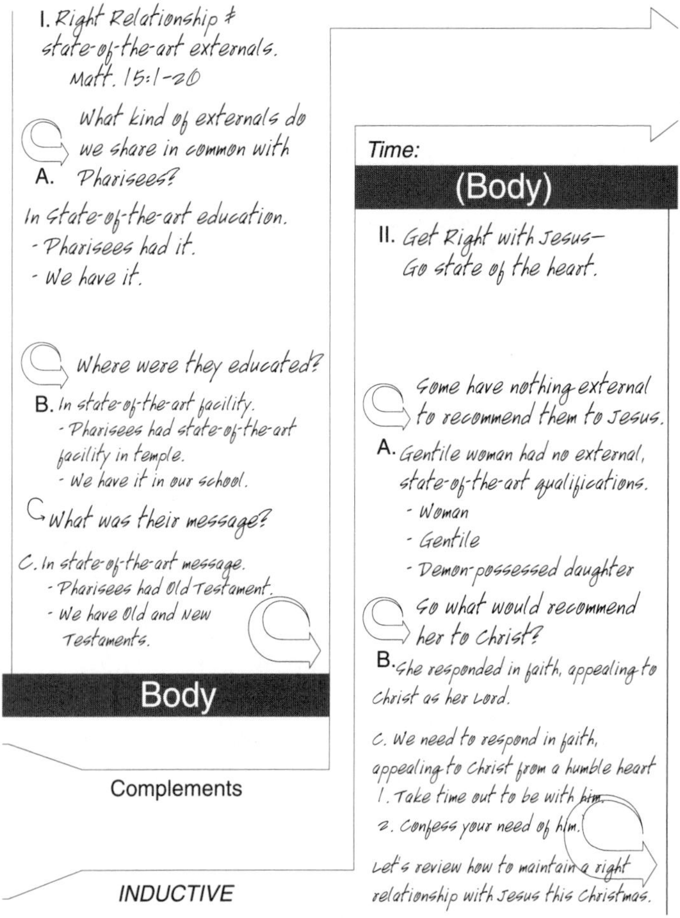
I. Right Relationship & state-of-the-art externals. Matt. 15:1-20
What kind of externals do we share in common with Pharisees?
A. In state-of-the-art education.
- Pharisees had it.
- We have it.
Where were they educated?
B. In state-of-the-art facility.
- Pharisees had state-of-the-art facility in temple.
- We have it in our school.
What was their message?
C. In state-of-the-art message.
- Pharisees had Old Testament.
- We have Old and New Testaments.
Body
Complements
INDUCTIVE
Time:
(Body)
II. Get Right with Jesus— Go state of the heart.
Some have nothing external to recommend them to Jesus.
A. Gentile woman had no external, state-of-the-art qualifications.
- Woman
- Gentile
- Demon-possessed daughter
So what would recommend her to Christ?
B. She responded in faith, appealing to Christ as her Lord.
C. We need to respond in faith, appealing to Christ from a humble heart
1. Take time out to be with him.
2. Confess your need of him.
Let's review how to maintain a right relationship with Jesus this Christmas.
Figure 5.2

ideas of what "being alert" means. Don't flag any of them as being right or wrong interpretations at the outset. Simply probe at least one consequence of living with the attitude, "Hey, I'm saved and that's good enough for me. I believe in eternal security—once saved always saved—I'm not going to sweat the fine points. Let the super-Christians work and suffer for their crown of righteousness. I'll be satisfied just to get in the gate!"

The objective is not to set up a straw man, or to caricature the worldly Christian, but to help the audience identify with this person. Enable them to say in their hearts, "Yeah, you know, he has a point. Is it really so awful just to be satisfied with heaven?" Then show what such a person stands to lose by failing to be alert. Show them in concrete images through stories that will touch the heart as well as the head. Effective use of illustrations will be covered in chapter 7. Such development keeps the story alive and fresh by challenging the audience to think along with you. Creating tension creates a need in the body, just as it does in the introduction. With time and a little imagination preachers can create interesting paths. Just be sure the paths lead back to the "right way" before time runs out.

The outline points are still logically necessary to define what it means to be "spiritually alert," only the approach to the definition is more creative. Exploring alternative answers creates tension. The audience will be tense because they will be shown a small but disturbing part of their face in the mirror of Scripture. They will see how distorted their perception of truth has been and how that distorted perception can lead to disaster. The tension relaxes as the true understanding of spiritual alertness becomes evident, and they learn how that awareness can start a process of spiritual transformation that is both exciting and rewarding.

You have completed the body of the sermon. The first part (introduction) flows seamlessly into the second part (body). The transitions between the main points of the body dovetail nicely into one another, revealing thoughtful design and integration of individual thoughts.[2]

There remains one major section left to develop: the conclusion. You can take the people on a grand trip to heaven and back, but you don't want to crash and burn on re-entry. The conclusion is your landing gear. In chapter 6 we will learn how to construct a conclusion in such a way as to bring the sermon in safely and smoothly and leave passengers looking forward to the next ride.

Chapter summary:

Body and transitions

1. Write a brief transition statement linking the intro-duction to the first main point.
2. Decide on the real question(s) the congregation is asking.
3. Construct the homiletical outline so that one point flows seamlessly into the next.
4. Carefully use subpoints to develop the main points.
5. Make sure transitions among the main points of the outline show their relationship to one another.

2. There is a tendency to think each sermon must have three points. In fact, a sermon can have as many points as it needs. In general the text reveals about this number.

6

Building the Landing Gear:
Conclusions

What Do I Do When I Arrive
At My Destination?

T minus six.

In the third structural step we strive for clarity.

The conclusion forms the third and final major section of the sermon. On our rocket the body is the longest stage, the introduction, shorter, and the conclusion is the most brief. After long labor over the introduction and body the preacher may feel the sermon is all but over and pay little attention to the conclusion.

This temptation must be resisted, however, if we want to bring our sermons in for a smooth landing. Churches are littered with debris from sermons that self-destructed as they were attempting to land. They took off without a hitch and soared for thirty glorious minutes above the biblical landscape, only to crash between the pulpit and the nearest exit.

There are several reasons for this disaster. Some run out of gas. We have all heard speakers who sputter out a few lame "concluding remarks." The sermon wobbles, then plummets, desperately seeking a last-minute updraft of inspiration—but the preacher too late realizes that the place for improvisation is the playground, not the pulpit.

> And now, in conclusion, just let me say, that, uh in summary, I'm sure you would agree with me in saying that the apostle's words are an encouragement to us all, I'm sure, and now, well, may the Lord richly bless this to our hearts and mindsletuspray . . .

Or the preacher may run out of time.

> Well, the old clock on the wall is a mean taskmaster this morning, so let me just quickly say in conclusion that we will pick up here next time in the travels of the great apostle . . .

Whatever the excuse the results are always the same. The audience leaves feeling cheated—abandoned to a listless contemplation of how to draw the strings together to capture the thought. They may now feel that half-conscious itch mentioned in chapter 4. They now long to be reminded of where they are and what they are to do now. There is a natural longing in all people for completion and unity. They are uncomfortable with fragmentation, or a sense of incompletion. Just try to imagine playing the first three notes of Beethoven's Fifth Symphony:

> Da–Da–Da– . . .

You have to complete it, don't you? You long to hear that fourth and final "DA!" If it isn't played, you will sing it to yourself. The same thing happens with well–known phrases:

To be or not to be: That is the . . .

Automatically the reader must finish the sentence with "question." Completing the idea achieves wholeness and, in some small way, harmony.

In a good conclusion we say to the audience: "Let's briefly review what we have discovered on our trip and see what our next step should be." The conclusion distills the truth of the sermon; its emphases are on review and exhortation. When done well, the conclusion exerts tremendous influence on the hearers, reminding them to act on what they have discovered to be true.

Smooth, solid landings

Think of a conclusion as the landing gear on a space shuttle. Without it the sermon only grinds to a stop, at best. With it passengers come in for a smooth landing that will help them appreciate the trip even more.

Here are some tips on several ways to build a strong conclusion (and avoid a shaky one):

1. Repeat and restate the homiletical central proposition and main points.
2. Exhort to an application that already has been made.
3. Conclude with an apt quotation.
4. Quote a brief and fitting poem.
5. Accent with a short story or illustration.
6. Appeal to the magic "What if . . . ?"
7. Use a specially relevant prayer or benediction.
8. Spur individuals to a point of decision with a challenge or dare.
9. Follow a challenge with a promise.
10. Use a meaning-filled hymn.
11. Any other creative concept.

Repeat and restate

Repetition (saying the same thing using the same words) aids memory, while *restatement* (saying the same thing using different words) aids understanding. When preaching from Matthew 15 the preacher should repeat the central proposition several times after he introduces it in the second main point. If the audience forgets everything else, they should remember to, "Get right with Jesus—Go state of the heart." The line is so important, it is the last thing said before we pray. But simple repetition is not enough; the preacher needs to restate the central proposition to enhance understanding:

> When it comes to worshiping Jesus, the issue isn't state of the art. He isn't concerned about where you bought your suit. He isn't impressed by where you studied or for how long. It doesn't matter to him if you are a junior partner in your firm or the janitor who cleans the toilets. What counts with the Lord Jesus is the state of your heart—Do you recognize him and acknowledge him as Lord? If you want to get right with Jesus, then know this: He wants your heart—all of it, nothing held back.

The same rule applies for the main points. If the sermon has been constructed so that the message flows logically from one point into the next, then a review of the main points will cement that structure in the congregation's memory. They will leave with the central proposition *and* the basic outline of the message as well. The net effect should be that they will be able to think through the sermon from beginning to end. The more they recall the more likely they are to apply what they have learned.

Exhort to an application already made

Exhortation should follow a review of the central proposition and main points. This is not new material, but a general review of specific applications made earlier in the message. For example, if preaching from 1 Peter 3:7 on how husbands are to treat their wives in an understanding manner, you may have spent half the message suggesting specific ways for husbands to do just that. The concluding reminder, however, must be more general:

> Gentlemen, if you value your relationship with the Lord, then value your wife. If you would have the Lord listen to your prayers, then listen to your wife. In short, treat her as you would have the Lord treat you.

Use an apt quotation

Quotations should not require explanation but should capture the thought in clear and vivid words. An apt quotation provides more than mere window dressing for an idea. As in the case of any other kind of illustrative material, use a quote only when it will enable the audience to comprehend the truth more readily. As a boy one of the authors spent many afternoons roosting in the gently swaying boughs of an enormous hackberry tree in his back yard, looking for pictures in the clouds. When a really great cloud formation drifted by he called out to his sister to see the giant pirate ship or the mountain in the sky. But he found out early on that he couldn't just say, "Look, don't you see it? It's right in front of you!" He had to define it for her, show her where the mast was and point out the curve of the sails.

Finding pictures in the clouds is a bit like seeing a truth in the Bible. You have seen the truth in your text and you are trying to help the audience to see the same image. It's as if your idea hovers before the audience like a cloud, the edges a bit fuzzy, a skitch out of focus. The carefully chosen quote traces the rim of thought with iridescent light, adding color and definition and precision. It helps the congregation say to themselves, "Aha! Now I see!"

On the desirability of studying God's Word:

What Robert Frost said of poetry we would say of studying
the Bible: "It begins in delight and ends in wisdom."

On adolescent love:

When it comes to young love I would have to agree with
H. L. Mencken when he described it as "the triumph of
imagination over intelligence."

On the spirit of the Old Testament law:

To paraphrase Grotius, God's law "obliges us to do what is
proper, not simply what is just."

On the need to embrace one's individuality in Christ:

Unfortunately, life for most men is, as Clifton Fadiman
said, "a search for the proper manila envelope in which to
get themselves filed."

On materialism:

Franz Werfel sums up the essence of materialism when he
says it is nothing but "organized emptiness of the spirit."

Quote from poetry

You can use a brief and fitting poem in much the same
way as a quotation. The challenge here is twofold: (1) to
choose truly good poetry, and (2) to recite or read it well.
So much of the poetry included in modern anthologies, especially those labeled "Christian,"[1] is trite or sentimental

---

1. One notable exception is *Eerdmans' Book of Christian Poetry*, edited by
Pat Alexander (Grand Rapids: Eerdmans, 1981). Though the book is lamentably
brief and it's scope fairly narrow, the poetry is excellent, and it is beautifully
illustrated.

and unworthy of private reading, much less public recitation. The only way to tell truly good poetry from the saccharine drivel that leaves fingers sticky from turning the page is to read great poets regularly. The local librarian can guide those uncertain about how to find the great poets into the wonder-filled country where, Thomas Gray notes, "Thoughts breathe and words burn."

It won't take long, after reading authentic poetry, to recognize the impostors. Good poetry does not restrict the preacher to obscure Shakespearean sonnets or cryptic passages from William Blake (Never confuse depth with obscurity). For example, the reader of great poetry can visit an orchard "After Apple–Picking" with Robert Frost. Louis Untermeyer described this work as "a poem of reality. "After Apple–Picking" has the enchantment of a lingering dream."[2] You also may wander down the gritty streets of "Chicago" in the company of Carl Sandburg or carry a frozen burden with a grizzled Yukon prospector in Robert W. Service's classic "The Cremation of Sam Magee."

Finding the poetry is one thing; reading it well is something else again. You have the option of either reading it off the page or of reciting it from memory. Reading is relatively safe, since the words are there before your eyes. Still, you want to maximize your eye contact with the audience, glancing to the page only when it is appropriate to the flow of thought. While most of us may shrink in fear from reciting a memorized piece, there is no denying that reciting from memory has more impact, simply because the preacher may concentrate on people, rather than a piece of paper.

Try memorizing a stanza (four lines or so) from a favorite poem. Then, read the stanza to a friend while looking at

2. Introduction and commentary, in Robert Frost, *Pocket Anthology of Robert Frost's Poems*, enl. ed., edited by Louis Untermeyer (New York: Washington Square, 1966), 228.

the words on the page. Next, recite the stanza from memory (go slowly here), looking directly into the eyes of the friend. There's more communication going on the second time around, isn't there? It is natural to feel awkward when reciting something for the first time while looking straight into someone's eyes. That awkward feeling is a good sign—evidence of interpersonal contact. With time and practice, God can transform that awkwardness into confidence. He doesn't want us to be feeble and afraid when we proclaim the good news. He wants bold ambassadors who will look men and women in the eye and tell them, without flinching, that if they are in Christ Jesus he loves them more than they can know.[3]

Just a little time invested in memorizing a poem can pay big dividends. The congregation will engage these ideas. Rather than just hearing words, they will begin to see, perhaps even to experience, the pictures painted with words. So many of us have simply forgotten how to imagine. A finely wrought poem can unlock the sense of wonder that lies rusting in the heart. But the poem itself will not suffice, just as a beautiful key is useless in the hands of one who is unfamiliar with its function. It takes some practice to learn to use a key in a rusty lock. Force it, and the key breaks, forever shutting you out.

We must read fine poetry well if we expect it to unlock hearts. Learn to read it well by rehearsing. Go over the poem twenty or thirty times if necessary to visualize the action and setting. The principle is, the more deeply you immerse yourself in the poem, the more likely your audience is to experience the truth you are trying to convey.

Accent with a story or illustration

A short story or illustration often provides the appropriate accent for an effective conclusion. The story should

3. See Eph. 6:19, 20.

capture the mood, as well as the essence of the truth to be conveyed. Be careful to choose a story with a balance of content and suitable emotional appeal. The temptation is to "juice up" an otherwise dry sermon with an emotional story that tugs at the heart but has little to do with the message.

To *manipulate* is to unfairly alter a situation to meet selfish needs. When we try to get people to respond through an appeal to their emotions alone, then we are manipulating them—even if we are trying to get them to do something good. An appeal to the emotions is good as long as the appeal is natural and unforced and as long as we balance it with a thoughtful consideration of the content of the message. Emotion should grow out of the story as a delicate rose emerges from the soil. Ignoring emotion leaves the sermon a barren field; import emotion artificially, and the field grows only plastic flowers. If the emotion is in the story cultivate it, but with the following rule in mind: Always leave your audience knowing you had more to give. Never exhaust the emotions in a story. Never lose control.

Appeal to the magic "What if . . . ?"

In life, and surely in the applications to sermons, don't let "the way things are" prevent exploration and eventual discovery of "the way things could be."

The "way things are" can be discouraging. A self-critical pastor examines life and ministry and thinks: "I'm no Paul. I'm no Peter. I'm not even a Mark. In fact, I feel more like Judas a lot of the time. I'm tired of failing, of selling out in little ways. I honestly doubt that I'll ever be any more than I am right now." Even if you never come right out and say the words, if you as pastor feel that way, chances are that both you and some people before you need a magic "What if . . . ?", especially at the end of a heavy sermon. "What if . . . ?" holds out realistic hope, not wishful thinking.

What if we could live a consistently victorious life? It's possible!

What if we sat down with our wives at the end of the day and said, "I love you. Tell me about your day"?

What if we respected our teenagers' privacy so that we refused to enter their rooms until we knocked first?

What if you did a secret favor for one of your employees.

The "What if . . . ?" approach throws down the gauntlet. It challenges to action as it appeals to the imagination. "What if . . . ?" compels the listener to consider the possibility that things could change in their lives if they would only act on the truth they have heard.

Involve the prayer and benediction

Most of us close a sermon with a prayer and a benediction. More often than not, the prayer is improvised. There is an aversion to constructing prayers, out of a fear that planned prayers sound artificial, pretentious, and therefore insincere. Some Protestant traditions have adopted an antiliturgical posture, partly out of a desire to keep prayers honest and organic. But suppose we have been invited, literally and physically, into the throne room of the Lord God. The engraved invitation arrives on Sunday morning:

<blockquote>
You are summoned
to attend an audience
with the King of all kings
one week from today
at precisely 11:55 a.m.
</blockquote>

𝔜𝔬𝔲 𝔪𝔞𝔶 𝔢𝔵𝔭𝔯𝔢𝔰𝔰 𝔶𝔬𝔲𝔯 𝔥𝔢𝔞𝔯𝔱
𝔬𝔫 𝔞𝔫𝔶 𝔰𝔲𝔟𝔧𝔢𝔠𝔱 𝔶𝔬𝔲 𝔡𝔢𝔢𝔪 𝔞𝔭𝔭𝔯𝔬𝔭𝔯𝔦𝔞𝔱𝔢
𝔱𝔬 𝔟𝔯𝔦𝔫𝔤 𝔟𝔢𝔣𝔬𝔯𝔢 𝔥𝔦𝔰 𝔐𝔞𝔧𝔢𝔰𝔱𝔶.

𝔗𝔥𝔢 𝔏𝔬𝔯𝔡 𝔴𝔦𝔩𝔩 𝔯𝔢𝔠𝔢𝔦𝔳𝔢 𝔶𝔬𝔲
𝔦𝔫 𝔱𝔥𝔢 𝔊𝔯𝔢𝔞𝔱 𝔗𝔥𝔯𝔬𝔫𝔢 𝔕𝔬𝔬𝔪.

One week to prepare . . . surely we would consider carefully and even write out what we would say to our Creator. It would be impertinent, not to mention foolish, to approach the divine Sovereign assuming we could say whatever happened to pop into our head at the moment. And yet every Sunday we tend to give much more attention to what we will say to our congregation than to what we will say to the Lord God. It is no more a sin to carefully prepare a closing prayer than it is to prepare a sermon, but it is at least as great a sin not to. There are many collections of prayers to use as resources.

The Bible itself is the greatest source of all for great prayers and benedictions. It has inspired innumerable compendiums of prayers and meditations on the Lord. Thomas à Kempis' *Imitation of Christ* is one of the finest. *The Book of Common Prayer*,[4] used by churches of the Anglican communion, has had a great influence on English literature and provides a treasure house of exquisite prayer. *Eerdmans' Book of Famous Prayers*[5] contains a fairly broad range of reverent and exquisitely penned prayers.

Commit some favorites to memory and use them when appropriate. Other prayers may inspire your own expression. We have inherited a rich heritage of prayers from some of the most godly men and women (and sometimes children) of the ages. Unhappily, most of that invocational

---

4. The definititive edition is published by Oxford University Press.
5. Veronica Zundel, ed. (Grand Rapids: Eerdmans, 1984).

gold sits collecting dust, while we rummage through a few stock phrases, pull out some last–minute tattered clichés and drape them across the exposed back of an otherwise dignified sermon. They dishonor the King, and are unworthy of his ambassadors. Try writing out or memorizing (or even reading) a prayer next Sunday and see how the Lord works.

Challenge or dare to action

A challenge or a dare can electrify a congregation, spurring them to a point of decision. The apostle Paul challenged young Timothy:

> In the presence of God and of Christ Jesus, who will judge the living and the dead, and in view of his appearing and his kingdom, I give you this charge: Preach the Word; be prepared in season and out of season; correct, rebuke and encourage—with great patience and careful instruction. [2 Tim. 4:1–2]

The challenge should be a final direct appeal to do—to act on the knowledge received in the message. Again, the appeal is not so much focused on the particulars of the action as it is a call to arms in the name of Christ:

> God challenges us in the name of Jesus Christ: Let go of this world and take hold of God.

> God's Word dares us to trust him with all we have.

> I challenge you to take time out this Christmas to worship him alone. See if you don't discover the Christmas you've been looking for all this time.

> I challenge you ladies—Find a creative way to honor your husband this week; something you've never done before.

Be bold in Christ. I dare you to find one person this week—
a neighbor, a friend, a relative—and speak to him or her
about Jesus.

There is a solemnity about a challenge of this kind. Use
it when your congregation is a little shaky in their faith and
they need a strong exhortation. You are saying in effect,
"Try the truth of the Lord on for size; live it out in obedience and see if he doesn't work on your behalf."

Remember God's promises

A promise is almost always good following a challenge.
People need the verbal reassurance that God will not aban-
don them in an enterprise of faith when it is taken up for
his glory.

Jesus tells us to stop worrying about everyday needs; the
Lord provides for the birds of the air—He will take care of
his children, too.

Stand up for the name of Jesus Christ. He has promised
never to leave you, never to forsake you.

If you have placed your trust in Christ for salvation you
need never fear hell again. Heaven is yours.

Promises are double-edged swords. They can be positive or negative.

If you continue to reject the free gift of salvation in Christ,
then you must inherit the dark promise of God—hell and
eternal death.

If we as Christians continue in this sin, God promises he
will discipline us. He will chastise us by allowing us to have
our own way, suffering the consequences. Repent and turn
back to him while there is still time.

Use hymns to close

Consult with your worship leader, or if you are flying solo get a good book on the history of hymns[6] and work the story of the closing hymn into the concluding remarks when appropriate. This prepares the audience mentally and emotionally to enter into a final, thoughtful expression of the message in song. A well-chosen closing hymn will help them remember the sermon when it flows naturally out of the message and reinforces the theme of the morning worship. It's also the first small step toward application as it permits a public affirmation of the truth just discovered in the sermon.

On 1 Peter 3:13–4:6:

> We suffer for our faith, and yet we must never hesitate to proclaim the gospel with courage and compassion. We are not alone in our distress. Christians have sustained great loss for the cause of Christ from the first century on. The year 1744 was a year much like our own for Christians. In England it was a year filled with great tension, confusion, and unrest. The Wesleys and their Methodist followers were persecuted because they were accused of trying to overthrow the throne. What we are about to sing was the opening hymn in a collection published that year entitled *Hymns for Times of Trouble and Persecution*. It was written by Charles Wesley as much for you and me as for the beleaguered Christians in the eighteenth century. And his message will ring just as true for future generations of Christians: "Ye Servants of God, Your Master Proclaim."[7]

Avoiding a shaky landing

The number of different and effective ways to conclude a message is limited only by imagination and the time it

6. A good one is Donald P. Hustad and George H. Shorney, Jr., *Dictionary-Handbook to Hymns for the Living Church* (Carol Stream, Ill.: Hope, 1978).
7. Adapted from Hustad and Shorney, *Dictionary-Handbook*, 28.

takes to weave them into the sermon. There are, however, a few potholes to avoid as you bring your sermon in for a landing:

Sidestep interest lags (yours and theirs)

Sustain a high level of interest in the congregation by maintaining your own energy level as you conclude. If preaching twice or more on a Sunday morning, it is particularly easy to "shut down" early. At no point in the sermon is it safe to go on auto-pilot. Hold concentration to maintain a high energy level, and you will hold the audience to the last syllable.

Ban long conclusions

The conclusion should be brief, on average around 5 percent to 10 percent of the message. The conclusion for a thirty-minute sermon, then, should be about one and one-half to three minutes. The conclusion is not the place for the climax to the sermon. The climax may come in the last point of the body, but the conclusion should plainly and briefly review and exhort to action.

Do not hint that you are about to conclude when you are not

Do not review the main points and proposition, only to launch into another unexpected point. This promises a wrap-up; so does slowing the pace. When the engines are cut and the landing gear lowered, passengers expect the preacher to set it down, not circle the field for another 15 minutes. An unmistakable impression accompanies the words, "In conclusion . . ." Don't say it. Don't announce the conclusion at all. Simply review the proposition and/or main points. Exhort me to do what God wants me to do, then let me go home and do it.

Evade monotony

Don't conclude each sermon in the same way. If one conclusion revolves around a poem, the next might use a good quote next week. Memorize a new benediction. Experiment. Not every effort will hit a homerun, and some will flat blow it, but at least you won't be guilty of giving less than your best. Taking some chances teaches what it means to trust God when you are scared to death and it's all on the line for his name's sake. Of course, you don't stand to lose much if you always play it safe, but then there isn't much to gain either.

Escape apology

Most apologies are for going overtime. Sometimes the preacher slips up through carelessness, but usually overtime sermons are deliberate. No one stands with a gun at your back forcing you to go past high noon. Most of the workers in the congregation are used to getting paid extra for working late. Congregations trust preachers to respect their time by finishing on time. Do not abuse that trust.

But we can hear the righteous rumbling, "What if the Spirit leads me to go long?" While you certainly want to be sensitive to the Holy Spirit's direction, beware that when "on a roll" it's easy to mistake the leading of the Spirit with a bloated sense of self-importance. The sound of your own voice can be as intoxicating as cheap wine, and just as dangerous to good judgment.

The Spirit will not lead anyone to consistently disregard the established time limits of a sermon. Long–winded sermonizing is nothing more than anarchy and sloth masquerading under the thin veneer of pious sensitivity. Apologies in this case ring hollow. Deny these self–serving pats on the back for having been over–zealous for the Lord. Save breath and apologies for those rare occasions when they are truly needed.

Shun trite, hackneyed conclusions

Trite conclusions grow like a dirty slush ball. They are filled with the common stuff of the road. Their impact leaves listeners cold and dripping—and looking for a fresh change of thought. Mark Twain said, "The difference between the right word and the almost right word is the difference between lightning and the lightning bug." The one

DEDUCTIVE

Purpose

Time:

(Body)	Conclusion
II. *Get Right with Jesus— Go state of the heart.*	1. *Don't count on externals Since even the best won't guarantee a right relationship with God.*
Some have nothing external to recommend them to Jesus.	
A. *Gentile woman had no external, state-of-the-art qualifications.* - *Woman* - *Gentile* - *Demon-possessed daughter*	
So what would recommend her to Christ?	*Since they don't—*
B. *She responded in faith, appealing to Christ as her Lord.*	2. *Develop a heart relationship with Jesus this Christmas.* - *Take time with him.* - *Confess your need of him.* - *Get right with Jesus* - *Go state of the Heart.*
C. *We need to respond in faith, appealing to Christ from a humble heart* *1. Take time out to be with him.* *2. Confess your need of him.*	
Let's review how to maintain a right relationship with Jesus this Christmas.	

Figure 6.1

illuminates the world with power and sparkle, while the other reveals the backside of a bug. I'll trade 10,000 lightning bug words for one lightning bolt. But it is the same old problem—lightning bugs are easy to catch. "Almost right" words come cheap. Look a little harder and, every once in awhile, God will let you grab a little lightning and put it in a jar.

Remember the conclusion aims at increased clarity. A congregation can see the truth more clearly with a review of the central proposition and perhaps even the main points. Explore different ways to review and reinforce. Your only limits are the boundaries of your imagination.

The conclusion for the sermon on Matthew 15:1–28 looked like this:

Conclusion
1. State of the art externals do not guarantee a right relationship with God.
2. We will get right with God when we see him for who he is and bow our hearts before him in humble dependence.
3. Remember, we do not worship the service of our Lord; we worship the Lord of our service.
4. Take time out this Christmas to get right with God by bowing before him alone and worshiping him in the quietness of your heart.
5. Get right with Jesus—Go state of the heart.

The landing gear is designed and the basic structure of the message (introduction, body, and conclusion) complete. Summarize the conclusion on your chart. Notice there are only two points. Those are to remind you that you need to review and exhort—briefly!

Now we are ready to add the detail that will enhance the journey. Part 3 will concentrate on support materials and style in the manuscript. If you have never developed a systematic method of gathering and filing support materials, and especially if you have never discovered the joy and security that comes with a well prepared manuscript, get ready to enter one of the most enjoyable phases of sermon preparation.

Chapter summary:

Conclusions

1. Review at least the central proposition and perhaps even the main points.
2. Exhort the congregation to act on the particulars revealed in the body.
3. Experiment with different ways to review and exhort, such as poetry and quotations.

Part **3**

Enhancing the Journey

7

Making the Journey Memorable: Supporting Material

How Do I Keep the Trip Interesting and Enjoyable?

T minus five.

Focus on interest and clarity in supporting materials.

The ship stands complete and fueled; its superstructure is solid. You know where you want to go and what to do upon arrival. There's just one problem: The sermon body, where you will spend at least 70 percent of the time, looks as empty as the cargo hold of a flying fortress. Its walls have been buttressed with steely thought and welded together to withstand the resistance of strong intellectual turbulence—but there's no place to sit. Our sermons may be airtight, exegetically safe, and theologically invincible, but if we don't make the ride a pleasant one people will find another pilot. A power sermon does more than get people somewhere; it takes them in such a way that they want to go again. Support materials can make the trip delightful and beneficial. They tap into the right side of the brain, clarifying foggy associations and connections.

Young children rely on anything that helps them communicate their ideas—stories, anecdotes, quotes, sticks, rocks—whatever lies at hand. As adults, now, we regard those natural elements of persuasion as foreign matter, alien fragments of a world before formal education. We tend to can all the wonderfully imaginative ways we once got points across, label them "support materials," and store them on a top shelf, out of sight behind the pickled beets. What happened?

At about age six, most of us entered a formal classroom where numbers suddenly became quite important. The introduction of abstract thinking, logical constructions, and other left-brain grownup hookeries[1] render the visceral world sadly and irretrievably explainable. Mysteries that needle children into asking such questions as, "Why is the sky?" receive bloodless answers that leave no secrets to challenge the imagination.

Why must we teach children that the only good mystery is a solved mystery? Solutions are fine as far as they go, but solving the mystery lets the fun out of the balloon. "Once you've solved the mysteries you'll be grown up and mature," becomes the unspoken message a child hears. Unfortunately, such "maturity" is often nothing but a smoke screen to hide a shriveled imagination. Continual interruption of fantasy with fact throws a blotter on the imagination even in preaching and teaching. Logical analysis, cold intellectual theories, and mechanical dissection of the text bore and can be lethal to any passionate embrace of the truth. But, like plants withered by inattention, the long dor-

1. *Hookeries* is a coinage—the allusion is to Captain Hook in "Peter Pan." Hook is emblematic of all that is bad about being grown-up. His is a sort of reductionist worldview that eliminates the "unnecessary stuff" like imagination.

mant seed of imagination will revitalize with a little water and careful nurture. In this chapter we will discover how to do just that.

Powerful sermons mix a bit of subjective seasoning into the homiletical stew to flavor the objective meat and potatoes. The amount of "seasoning" needed depends on the kind of text you are preaching. A narrative text may already contain all the seasoning it needs.

Think of a father and two-year-old daughter out in the yard on Easter morning. Brightly decorated eggs lie hidden all around, but the excited child still needs some help to find them. Dad's hints send her bounding off in the right direction; and she still feels the joy of discovering the rainbow–colored eggs on her own. Later on the phone to grandma the child relives the hunt. She describes the eggs' pretty colors and where she found each of them. She also includes how she felt—her subjective "analysis" of the event. Her natural joy splashes over the brim as she tints words as colorful as her new-found Easter eggs.

Children have a wonderful storytelling ability that naturally mixes the objective and the subjective. Their descriptions are never forced or artificial because they are born of immediate and quite personal experience. Neither are their stories antiseptically theoretical and analytical. A young child has neither the vocabulary nor the abstract reasoning ability to categorize an event as "exciting" or "joyful" or "wonderful." The little egg hunter doesn't *tell* her Grandmother how she feels; she *shows* those feelings by unfolding her little story in an exciting and joyful and wonderful way.[2] That narrative story requires no outside "support materials." The story itself is an extended illustration, with the remembered discovery of each egg further enhancing the effect of spontaneous and highly infectious joy.

2. Eugene L. Lowry develops the need for an objective/subjective mix in *The Homiletical Plot* (Atlanta: John Knox, 1980), 94.

A preacher with a good story—a passage that is already a narrative—doesn't need or want much outside support illustrations and anecdotes. The narrative passage accomplishes the task of illustrating a truth. If the text exposited is already a narrative, additional stories will detract by interrupting the flow of the biblical story. At most the preacher may want to include a parallel contemporary story, to help show the listener's connectedness to the biblical characters and their struggles.

Not every passage we preach lends itself quite so easily to the story form. Those more didactic texts, including most of the Epistles and much of the Old Testament Law, need support in the same way a skeleton needs flesh and blood to be "embraceable." It's hard to hug a bunch of bones.

"Illustration is a psychological necessity,"[3] said John Broadus. As "illustration" Broadus includes the full range of support materials that explain, prove, adorn, or in any other way undergird the text so that we better understand it, embrace it, and apply it.

Good supporting materials provide focused answers for the focusing questions: "What does it mean?" "Is it really true?" "So what difference does it make?" (see pp. 50–54).

We see models of each type of supporting material in the Bible. Jesus told parables of the kingdom to help people understand what the kingdom is like. He was answering the first focusing question, because the popular view of the kingdom and the King was so foggy it needed fundamental correction. Jesus was giving the nation new spectacles so they could correct their spiritual vision. The parables of the kingdom helped people see and understand the truth.

Paul used supporting materials to help prove a point and so answered the second focusing question. In his allusion

3. John Broadus, *On the Preparation and Delivery of Sermons* (New York: Harper and Row, 1944), 196.

in 1 Corinthians 9:24 to the Isthmian games held near Corinth he tried to persuade his readers to exercise self-discipline by reminding them of their future reward. His argument went like this: Both the Christian and the athlete compete for a reward. If the athlete is willing to discipline himself to win a leafy crown that is sure to shrivel, how much more should Christians be willing to exercise self-discipline in the quest for a crown of unfading glory? James addresses the same focusing question in 3:6 when he uses the illustration of a small fire to help convince his readers of the blistering menace of an uncontrolled tongue.

Jesus was a specialist in answering the third focusing question. He told many parables designed to help the listener apply the lesson of the parable. The good Samaritan (Luke 10:30–37) suggests how we ought to treat anyone who has a need—even if that person is a sworn enemy. In Mark 9:36–37 Jesus called a child to his side as an object lesson to teach the disciples about humility. "Welcome this child in my name, and it's the same as welcoming me and the one who sent me," He said. "Apply the truth in this way if you want to please me."

Let's explore just a few of the different kinds of support materials available to us: repetition; restatement; object lessons; stories or illustrations; explanation; testimony, and statistics.

Repetition

Repetition is "a good means of making or keeping impressions vivid, and almost the only means of keeping them unchanged," according to George Santayana.[4] Repeating key words, phrases, and even sentences aids memory. Often you will want to repeat verbatim the central proposition and main points to help them stick. Repetition

---

4. Quoted in Eugene E. Brussell, ed., *Webster's New World Dictionary of Quotable Definitions* (New York: Prentice Hall, 1988), 489.

is the suction cup tip on a toy arrow that sticks to the window of the mind. Repetition is the boomerang that brings an idea back to the hearer. Repeat a word, a phrase, a sentence, a sound, a movement often enough and people will remember. They will not be able not to remember: "Be a Churchill: 'Never give up.'"[5]

But why limit repetition to vocabulary? Repeat physical movements (stage position and gestures) to reinforce both the words and the structure of the sermon. For example, the first part of the sermon is a warning, and you deliver it from the right side of the pulpit. Each time you review that point you move back to the same place, and the audience will better remember the content of the point. They will also better remember where it fits into the overall structure of the message; repeating the physical position localized the point.

The same applies for gestures. Used strategically, a repeated gesture can make a point unforgettable. But hear a word of caution: repeated gestures can be dull, distracting, and even silly if they are overused. It is easy to fall into unintentional patterns of repetitive movement. To find out if you are guilty of "repetivitis" videotape yourself preaching. Play the tape at fast-forward speed. Repetitive movement will be immediately and painfully apparent. Here are some common movements, postures, and gestures to watch for:

- rising up on your toes to emphasize a point
- placing left and right fingertips together, then pressing and releasing (This maneuver resembles a spider doing pushups on a mirror.)
- rocking or swaying back and forth

5. From Winston Churchill's speech at Harrow School, Oct. 29, 1941. Quoted in *Bartlett's Familiar Quotations*, 15th ed., revised and enlarged (Boston: Little, Brown, 1980), 745.

- listing to port or starboard (Some of us lean as we preach.)
- a backhanded gesture
- pointing
- clapping hands or snapping fingers
- gesturing with one hand primarily, while the other is in the pocket
- sticking both hands in pockets
- grabbing or leaning on the pulpit
- looking down
- blinking
- licking lips
- scratching the head, face, or around the eyes
- smoothing the hair
- rubbing the chin, as in thoughtful contemplation
- pulling on the ear
- any random movement that serves no purpose

Remember that every movement and every sound adds to or detracts from a communicator's overall effectiveness. Unclutter delivery by eliminating repetitive movements that are nothing more than the random expression of nervous energy.

Restatement

When we restate a point or a proposition we say the same thing in other words. While repetition (saying exactly the *same* thing in the *same* way) aids memory, restatement fosters understanding. Restatement helps the audience see the truth from a different angle to understand and appreciate it more fully.

"Carpe Diem!"
"Seize the Day"
"Make the most of today—tomorrow is only a dream."

"Live the rest of this day as if the Lord were coming at midnight."

Object lessons

As Charles Ryrie says, "Object lessons are God's own idea (1 Cor. 10:11)."[6] Jesus used the pots and pans of life to illustrate principles that otherwise would have remained abstract and muddled. Flowers, birds, water, and children provided more than just fodder for sermon illustrations. They *were* the sermons. Lilies growing in a field were creations of God appareled in a regal splendor that outclassed Solomon himself. If God clothes the flowers so wonderfully, Jesus says, then why worry about what you will wear? Likewise, birds have nests and food, both signs of God's providential care, so why fret over what we, who are worth more than many sparrows, will eat tomorrow? One day, at the end of a long, hot walk, Jesus came to a well in Samaria. The water at the bottom of that well became a symbol for the water of life that he had come to offer the world. Jesus was a great observer of the world around him.

As God says in 1 Samuel 16:7, the truest evaluation of the world and all that is in it comes from the Creator. Kelly is a maturing artist whose works show depth and complexity. As she unveils some of her designs for her family she points out details of design and symmetry, nuance and textures. The uninformed eye would miss such things, but Kelly can help others appreciate her art pieces more deeply because she made them. The Lord is the supreme Artist. When he walked with his disciples in Galilee he was taking them on a tour of his great gallery of four–dimensional art. He could point out physical details and relationships between created things they had never seen before. His analysis of the three–dimensional world of length, breadth, and

6. Charles C. Ryrie, *Easy–to–Give Object Lessons* (Chicago: Moody Bible Institute, 1974), 2.

depth startled his followers. They had to learn that Jesus could see a deeper significance in creation because he made it.

Jesus' sensitivity to significance does not stop at the three-dimensional world. Since he is God, he plumbs the depths of the spiritual dimension. He saw in Peter a rock like faith. He saw a treasure in the heart of a widow with two small coins. The same principle was at work in the Old Testament when the Lord looked beyond the outward appearance of a small shepherd boy to see a king. Jesus consistently pierces the skin and gets right to the heart—whether the heart of a person or of a buttercup. His Word tells us what he has seen. He is able and willing to help us see more in his creation if we ask him to show us.

Story (or Illustration)

"Draw your chair up close to the edge of the precipice and I'll tell you a story."[7]

F Scott Fitzgerald was right; a good story invites us to the edge of a precipice. There we may be enshrouded in a dense cloud of fear with Anne Franke or breathe deeply the autumn crisp air of freedom with Harriet Tubman or splash in crackling cold joy with Helen Keller. On the edge of the story precipice we can celebrate a wonderful party with a girl named Alice or fire the last shot from "Ol' Betsy" at the Alamo. A good story never bores. Balancing on the edge of a precipice brands the memory so that the story is often the only part of the sermon people will recall and try to recount to a friend. They will remember the illustration and forget the point illustrated. We need to make sure an audience makes the connection, so that when people remember the story they also will remember its lesson.

7. From "NoteBooks," in Edmund Wilson, ed., *The Crackup* (1945); quoted in John Bartlett, *Familiar Quotations*, 14th ed., edited by Emily Morrison Beck (Boston: Little, Brown, 1968), 1037.

So choose a story carefully—as carefully as if you were telling it to a king and the future of the kingdom depended on his understanding the point. Nathan had that very job (2 Sam. 12:1–14). He had to confront God's anointed king with his sin. Somehow he had to break through the months of denial and self-deception to get to David's heart. David's relationship with the Lord and the future of the nation hung in the balance.

Did Nathan approach his king with a graph illustrating the spiritual decline of the nation since his sin with Bathsheba? Did he offer a moralizing lecture of the bitter consequences of adultery? He told a simple little story that dramatically and positively altered the course of the nation and the life of its king. Stories have a way of sneaking up on a blind side and pulling the rug out from under the hearer. They slam home reality with unexpected force.

When we moralize by preaching at people in a superior and authoritarian tone, with tons of cold, hard facts to back us up, we are lobbing grenades into our own camp. No wonder defenses kick into red alert. Walls go up. Hearing aids turn off. An unspoken message goes out: "Don't tell me how bad I am. Encourage me so I don't have to stay as bad as I know I have been."

Still, there are rare times when we should not avoid a confrontation. Then we have to be very careful, as was Nathan, to know our audience at least as well as we know our story.

The most effective stories tap into the shared experience of the speaker and the audience. Most people identify with the experiences of loving another person or having been dealt with unfairly or losing a pet. Good illustrations reveal connections between these shared life experiences and a truth. As we help the audience see the parallels we should omit all the unnecessary and distracting details from the story. If a detail doesn't advance the story in a way that helps us see the truth more clearly or embrace it more readily, then we need to cut it.

We have to help the audience see the truth without allowing them the luxury of "watching" us present it. They must themselves participate in the story, as did David in 2 Samuel 12:5–6. Nathan's story electrified the whole man emotionally, and "David burned with anger." It also met him intellectually, for he understood the gross injustice inflicted on the poor man and his family. It ignited his will to act, and he commanded that the rich man, "must pay for that lamb four times over, because he did such a thing and had no pity." The best stories draw the congregation into an encounter with truth. Once they see that truth, be it a hard or a joyful truth, they simply cannot ignore it.

Think of it this way: A story places the audience at a $90,000 wedding, standing at the altar dressed in a $5000 gown, gazing into the eyes of the one they claim to love. It is time to say, "I do" or "I don't." They can no longer avoid it. They must either run from the truth or allow it to sweep them up in its power. Once they yield, once they face the truth they've been denying for so long, they will discover that their worst fears of being found out dissolve in the extravagant love of the Bridegroom.

Explanation

Explanation is indispensable when 2000 years separates us from the people and culture we are trying to understand. Alien ideas or practices need to be made clear with an explanation. How can we expect our audience to understand or even be acquainted with the Hebrew concept of the "Messiah"? By explaining what "Messiah" means we can help people understand that Jesus was uniquely qualified for his earthly role.

Unless listeners are versed in Roman antiquity they have no idea of the procedure for Roman adoptions, so they have little chance to grasp the significance of their position in, and identification with, Christ. We must explain it.

The disciples grew up understanding the symbolism of the Passover and its elements. We cannot assume that people have the foggiest notion of how the Passover helps us appreciate the Lord's sacrifice or the Lord's Supper. Explaining helps our people enter into the spirit of worship more fully.

Crucifixion was a thoroughly barbaric way of executing criminals, but our audiences have little knowledge of the horror, the dread, or the shame of the cross. When we explain Jesus' passion in graphic detail we help them appreciate his physical suffering for them.

Testimony

"A truthful witness gives honest testimony, but a false witness tells lies," observes Proverbs 12:17.

If the audience is asking the second focusing question ("Do I buy this?"), we may sense the need to usher in some recognized authority on the matter whose testimony will help persuade of the validity of our interpretation. Testimony rightly used can be a powerful tool of persuasion. It can add effectively to the emotional force of an argument and so move people to the decision we desire. Quoting Winston Churchill, for example, may galvanize the populace into a steely determination never to give in, even in the face of overwhelming odds.

Of course, we must choose the authority well. He has to be a recognized *and accepted* authority in the field. Quoting James Dobson on child rearing would probably be preferable to quoting Sigmund Freud or even Carl Jung on the same subject. Although all three are recognized in the field, the Christian community more readily accepts Dr. Dobson than either Freud or Jung.

However, we must be careful to remember that even the best testimony will only corroborate an argument; it can never improve its logic. When an argument, a thesis, or an interpretation of a text is weak no army of testimonials will "prove" your point. The argument ultimately stands or falls on its own merits, not because of external supports. In quoting even a recognized and accepted source in the field we are merely parroting someone else who agrees with us, but who could be wrong. Testimonials work rather like facts, which, as Aldous Huxley says, are "Ventriloquist's dummies. Sitting on a wise man's knee they may be made to utter words of wisdom; elsewhere, they say nothing, or talk nonsense, or indulge in sheer diabolism."[8] Use testimony to persuade but use it with discretion, knowing that you are prodding the heart more than the head. Do not rely on such testimony to make up for shoddy exegesis or theology.

Statistics

"When times are mysterious, serious numbers are eager to please."[9]

Stats are second cousins to "testimony" and the offspring of "facts." As in the case of testimony, statistics do not "prove" points; they merely marshal evidence for an impressive display. Statistics goose-step down the main street of our messages, blaring cold sermon notes from brass horns: "More than 50 percent of marriages today end in divorce!" "A recent poll shows that 94 percent of all Americans believe in God, and 69 percent believe in life after death!" What may we legitimately deduce from these statistics? We may infer that the rise in the divorce rate is the result of a failure to see marriage as a lifelong commitment. Or we could see it as indicative of a spiritual malaise

8. Aldous Huxley, quoted in Brussell, ed., *Quotable Definitions*, 188.
9. Paul Simon, "When Numbers Get Serious" from the album, *Hearts and Bones* (New York: Warner, 1983).

that is infecting the most cherished of our cultural institutions. Or both. We could see the high percentage of those who indicate a belief in God as either encouraging or terribly disquieting, given the moral cesspool in which we wade daily.

Numbers are nonpartisan, nonethnic, amoral abstractions—until we enlist them into an army of statistics. We need to remember that statistics are nothing more than mercenary numbers looking for a fight. Stats generally tend to reduce complex moral issues to black-and-white columns of uncompassionate, sharply articulated censure. Check out your statistics as you would medicine. Know the source, and use them sparingly. Over-the-counter stats should come with a warning: "Caution! Overdose leads to dementia. Side-effects include arrogance and impatience. May cause temporary blindness to other sides of the issue."

Finding support material

Once you have decided what kind of support material you need, you still have to find it. Here are a few suggestions for sources:

1. Draw from personal experience. Be careful not to abuse the privilege, or to expose family members to ridicule.
2. Draw from reading and viewing (be sensitive to community standards of acceptability. You may be dealing with meat sacrificed to idols).
3. Draw from listening (Garrison Keillor's radio essays . . . great music . . .).
4. Draw from imagination. Paint an imaginary story—letting listeners know it's imaginary.
5. Draw from illustration files and books. Avoid a "canned" feel to illustrations by retelling them in your own words.

6. Draw from resource people. Ask the congregation to help by sending you their favorite quotes and illustrations from books and magazines they read.

Now try jotting a short phrase or even a single word to indicate the support material on the model. You may wish to indicate support material in red ink so you can see at a glance how much material you have and where it is located in the sermon.

You have assembled all the parts of the interior of the sermon. Now we can sew it all together. Words are the threads we will use to connect all the pieces. The words we choose must be the right color, the right texture, and strong enough to hold the sermon together. If you settle for cheap words the sermon can unravel like an old sweater. Well-chosen words take more time, but the sermon will have a staying power and an everyday practicality that far exceeds the empty promises of dime store sermons. We are talking about style. In chapter eight we will find out how to use good style as we manuscript the sermon.

Chapter summary:

Supporting materials

1. Use vocal and physical repetition to help them remember your point.
2. Use restatement to help them understand your point.
3. Use object lessons to help them see your point.
4. Use stories to help them experience your point.
5. Use explanation to help them relate to your point.
6. Use testimony and statistics to help them accept your point.
7. Use the world as a support materials resource library.

8

Shaping the Interior: Manuscript

How Can I Make Sure the Style is Right for the Trip?

T minus four.

Good style adds to the clarity and interest of the sermon.

In chapter 7 we assembled all the remaining pieces of the sermon. The goal of this chapter is to arrange those pieces to fit the needs of our passengers. The result will be a customized manuscript that will uniquely suit the educational level and cultural situation of our congregation. In creating the manuscript we focus on style or word choice.

Remember as you flesh out the sermon that you are writing for the ear, not for the eye. You are writing words to be said, not read. Make them sticky—easy to grasp, hard to shake off. We can all improve our word choice. Even the wisest king on earth took pains to ferret out "just the right words" for his audience: "Not only was the Teacher wise, but also he imputed knowledge to the people. He pondered and searched out and set in order many proverbs. The Teacher searched to find just the right words, and what he wrote was upright and true" (Eccles. 12:9–10).

Maximum involvement—minimum effort. The right words invite an audience to participate in the gospel event with a minimum of mental strain. The higher their involvement the more likely they are to retain the truth. The longer they retain the truth the better the chance they will act on it.

But why go to all the trouble of manuscripting the entire sermon? Why not incorporate those "just right words" into the outline and have done with it? We feel the answer is compelling. The discipline of manuscripting the sermon affects delivery in two important ways: (1) It helps you stick to the sermon, and (2) it helps you remember the sermon. You will be less likely to wander, and you will remember the flow of thought better if you manuscript. While we do not advise attempting to memorize the manuscript, you will marvel at how many key phrases stick in mind with no conscious attempt at memorization when you deliver the message. Too, as you manuscript you tend to discover new word plays that often fail to surface in a simple outline.

The old adage is still true: "Good things happen when you begin to write." So it stands to reason that better things are bound to happen when you write more!

Here are a few stylistic suggestions as you begin to manuscript the introduction, the body, and the conclusion.

Write for clarity

"Have something to say, and say it as clearly as you can," stressed Matthew Arnold. "That is the only secret of style."[1]

1. Quoted in *Oxford Dictionary of Quotations*, 3d ed. (New York: Oxford University Press, 1979), 16.

Simplify complex thoughts

You can work hard on your sermon all week, but if you fail to write so that your audience understands, you have wasted your time. One of the meanest enemies of clarity is ambiguity. Haddon W. Robinson wrote, "A mist in the pulpit is a fog in the pew." He's right. One who cannot express a complex thought simply has not yet thought deeply enough. Ambiguity cloaks our thought in obscure language designed more to impress than to express. Some people feel that big words are a sign of a big intellect. Too often such fatty words are merely the discharge of a globular ego. We need to keep our words and our sentences lean and simple. The simpler the sentence the better it sticks. When you speak in simple sentences you keep company with the masters of the spoken word. Some of the most memorable prose in the English language are peppered with monosyllabic words. For example,

> Of 265 words in the Gettysburg Address 195 are one syllable.
>
> Between 70 and 78 percent of the words used by W. Somerset Maugham, Sinclair Lewis, Robert Lewis Stevenson, and Charles Dickens are one syllable.
>
> In Psalm 23 (KJV) 73 percent of the words are one syllable.
>
> In the Lord's Prayer 76 percent of the words are one syllable.
>
> In 1 Corinthians 13 some 80 percent of the words are one syllable.

Purge the polysyllabic profundities and embrace simple vibrant words. Adopt this prayer: "Lord, let me be monosyllabic today!"

Leave behind theological jargon

Of course, not all vague sermons are pompous exhibitions of flatulent garrulity; some sermons are ambiguous because of the preacher's isolation. At some point during the week we isolate ourselves from the world, ascend the tower and prepare the message. The trouble is that, in coming down from the ivy-covered tower, we drag a snarl of tangled jargon into the pulpit. The tendrils of jargon wrap themselves around our tongue, complicating simple ideas with esoteric gibberish. In short, we become "jargonauts." We study theology; we talk theology with kindred jargonauts; we do theology. Then, when we try to communicate on Sunday morning, we speak in an unknown tongue to the normal folks sitting in the pews. If they see our language as inaccessible how do you think they feel about the truth that language is trying to express? Maybe one of the reasons we don't see more fruit of the Spirit in our congregations is because we are sewing the seed in silk pouches. Let's unwrap the silk ribbon of jargon and let the plain word of God fall on good soil.

This is not to say that you should not educate a congregation. If the sermon deals with sanctification, then use the word. There is nothing wrong with expanding the theological vocabulary of the congregation. They need to know some basic terms to be conversant with current theological issues. But be careful to define the theological term, restate it and illustrate it so that the audience leaves with a true understanding of its meaning. Such is a *formal* development of a theological theme.

More *casual* references to the great theological truths (those we just mention in exposition) should echo the vernacular of the congregation. Rather than talking about "eschatology," speak of "future things." Rather than "the salvific purposes of God," tell me why Jesus died for me. Instead of lecturing on "ecclesiological disunity," tell me why we can't seem to get along in this church. And don't talk about "infralapsarianism" at all, unless it's in a joke that pokes fun at pointy-headed theologians. It takes time for the specialist to become free enough from the confines of jargon to talk to those outside the camp. Disentangle yourself from all this talk if you want people to understand the truth.

Be sensitive to connotative meaning

Another source of ambiguity is ignorance or insensitivity to the connotative value of a word. *Denotation* has to do with the *objective meaning* of a word. It's the bony side of your brain telling you that a *book* is "a printed work on sheets of paper bound together." The *connotative meaning*, however, has to do with a *subjective association* the word excites in the listener. It's the heart side of the brain—the poor inner-city kid who sees a book as a symbol of the lack of education that is holding him back. It all depends on the context.

> I may think of *freedom* when I talk about being *single*, but someone in the singles class at church may understand singleness as *bondage*—just the opposite of what I intend.
>
> Depending on the group, *abortion* will connote either a personal right or murder.
>
> The *cross* in one context connotes glory and victory, while in another it signifies pain and humiliation and shame.

Recognize and be sensitive to these hinge words—words that can swing either way depending on the context and the audience.

Some words and phrases, events and images universally connote either positive or negative associations. Most of these images span racial, social, and religious differences—

indeed, they span time itself, being found in the literature of cultures widely separated in time and space. *Home* in thirteenth-century China had the same positive connotative value as in twentieth-century Mexico.[2] For this reason, they are called *archetypes*.[3] The following is adapted from a list developed by Leland Ryken on archetypes in literature:[4]

The archetypes of the ideal experience

The human world: the community or city; images of communion, order, unity, friendship, love; marriage; the feast or meal; food, such as bread, milk, and meat, wine, and honey.

The animal world: a community of domesticated animals, usually a flock of sheep; a lamb, or one of the gentler birds, often a dove; a group of singing birds.

The vegetable world: a garden, grove, or park; a tree of life; the rose.

The inorganic world: a city, or one building or temple (for example, heaven portrayed as one house with many mansions, John 14:2 KJV); images of jewels and precious stones, often glowing and fiery; fire and brilliant light; burning that purifies and refines.

Water imagery: a river or stream; a spring of water; showers of rain; flowing water of any sort.

The forces of nature: the breeze or wind; the calm after a storm; the spring and summer seasons; the sun or the lesser light of the moon and stars; light, sunrise, day.

Miscellaneous: images of ascent; the mountain top or other images of height; images of birth and rebirth;

2. Even here we need to remain alert to the particular social environment in which we communicate. *Home* may be a familiar word, but an alien concept to a child who has never heard a story about a happy home, much less lived in one.

3. Leland Ryken defines an archetype as, "a symbol, character type, or plot motif that has recurred throughout literature . . . and whose meaning is universally understood." *The Literature of the Bible* (Grand Rapids: Zondervan, 1974), 22 and in the glossary under "archetype."

4. Ibid., 24, 25.

images of motion (as opposed to stagnation); images of freedom; musical harmony or singing.

The archetypes of unideal experience

The human world: tyranny or anarchy; isolation among people; the harlot, witch, and similar creatures; images of cannibalism, torture, mutilation (the cross, the stake, the scaffold, gallows, stocks, etc.); slavery and bondage; images of disease and deformity; sleeplessness or nightmare, often related to guilt of conscience.

The animal world: monsters or beasts of prey; the wolf (traditional enemy of the sheep), the tiger, the vulture, the cold and earth-bound serpent, and dragons.

The vegetable world: the sinister forest, often enchanted and under the control of demonic forces; the heath, wilderness, or wasteland, which is always barren and may be either a tropical place of great heat or a place of ice and intense cold.

The inorganic world: either the inorganic world in its unworked form of deserts, rocks, and wilderness, or its civilized form of cities of destruction and violence; the prison or dungeon; malignant fire that destroys and tortures instead of purifying.

Water imagery: the sea and all that it contains (sea beasts and water monsters), stagnant pools.

The forces of nature: the storm or tempest; the autumn and winter seasons; sunset, darkness, night.

Miscellaneous: images of descent; the valley; the underground cave or tomb; death; dry dust or ashes; images of rust and decay; images of stagnation or immobility; discordant sounds or cacophony.

Once you are familiar with these archetypal forms you can avoid using a powerfully connotative image in the wrong way. Conversely, the wise communicator will use archetypal images to reinforce the desired subjective response to a message.

Make abstract ideas concrete

Abstraction is second cousin to ambiguity and can be just as lethal to clear communication. An abstraction is any thought or expression that is "apart from" a particular instance or material object. People don't like to fiddle with them. "An American will tinker with anything he can put his hands on. But how rarely can he be persuaded to tinker with an abstract idea."[5] Why is that? It is because I relate to nothing in an abstraction. Nothing in an abstraction belongs to me. I have never smelled or tasted or heard or seen an abstraction.

Abstractions offer little more than the wisp of a thought—a vapor that floats before us for a moment then detonates with the force of a soap bubble when we try to reach out and touch it. Abstractions are ephemeral gremlin words that steal away the substance of concrete thought. Avoid them as you would the clammy embrace of a bloodless creature on Halloween night.

Turn instead to the brawn of concrete images. To be "concrete" is to solidify an abstraction, to make an abstraction sensate (capable of being apprehended through the senses). I can smell such concrete images as hot dogs or steaming apple pie or raw sewage on a hot day. I can taste the concrete images of ice cream so cold it makes your mouth hurt, pizza so hot it bubbles on your tongue, water so fresh it quenches the soul. Whoops! *Soul* isn't concrete is it? Yet, the image of the refreshing water says to me that the soul, whatever that is, can be refreshed in some way. So I come to understand a bit of the abstraction *soul* by understanding that it can be refreshed.

5. Leland Stowe, *They Shall Not Sleep*; quoted in John Bartlett, *Familiar Quotations*, 14th ed., Emily Morrison Beck, ed. (Boston: Little, Brown, 1968), 1046.

Why work so hard to come up with concrete images? Because the mind is an associative organ. We remember nothing in a vacuum, but only through a lightening fast association with related memories. The mind needs to see that an abstraction is *like* something in the "real" world (apologies to Plato). That's where simile and metaphor come in. A simile compares two things "like," "as," or "as if": "The demon's eyes glowed like hot embers on a winter night."

A metaphor makes the same comparison, but without the "like," "as," or "as if." Martin Luther penned two of the best: "A mighty fortress is our God, A bulwark never failing." Hold your Bible upside down—similes and metaphors come tumbling out! Look at the Song of Solomon, the Psalms, and Proverbs for some striking examples.

"The name of the Lord is a strong tower; the righteous run to it and are safe," (Prov. 18:10). What do you see when you see *the name of the Lord*? Solomon wanted us to respond subjectively to the abstract ideas of strength and security, so he chose a concrete image that objectified the abstraction. The *tower* is a metaphor that helps us "see" *the name of the Lord.*

Here are more abstractions (senses, emotions, etc.) expressed as similes and metaphors. After going over these, try some on your own—it won't take long before you will be thinking and expressing yourself more concretely. Ask yourself, "What is this abstract truth like?"

Metaphors

Confidence—"The wealth of the rich is their fortified city; they imagine it an unscalable wall" (Prov. 18:11).

Sight—"His legs are pillars of marble set on bases of pure gold" (Song of Sol. 5:15).

Taste—"Your navel is a rounded goblet that never lacks blended wine" (Song of Sol. 7:2).

Similes

Deceit—"Like a coating of glaze over earthenware are fervent lips with an evil heart" (Prov. 26:23).

Pugnacity—"Starting a quarrel is like breaching a dam; so drop the matter before a dispute breaks out" (Prov.17:14).

Smell—"His cheeks are like beds of spice yielding perfume" (Song of Sol. 5:13).

Sound—"A quarrelsome wife is like a constant dripping on a rainy day" (Prov. 27:15).

Stability—"[The man of God] is like a tree planted by streams of water, which yields its fruit in season and whose leaf does not wither" (Ps. 1:3).

Taste—"The words of a gossip are like choice morsels; they go down to a man's inmost parts" (Prov. 18:8).

Taste and touch—"For the lips of an adulteress drip honey, and her speech is smoother than oil; but in the end she is bitter as gall, sharp as a double–edged sword" (Prov. 5:3, 4).

Write for correctness

A good style will also be correct. The words chosen should fit the audience, the occasion, the subject, and the speaker. As noted above, we need to know our audience: Are they white collar, blue collar, or pink collar? Are they sophisticated, liberated, inebriated, distracted, or embalmed?

The occasion helps determine the style. Weddings don't sound like funerals—usually. People used to your regular Sunday morning service will remark on how "youth oriented" you sound as the high school commencement speaker. The appropriate style for an induction into office will be dignified and elegant. A campfire talk at a junior high retreat is loose, relaxed, and conversational.

Of course there is some spill over. High schoolers will be on the back pew on Sunday morning beside a few older folks from the retirement home. We preach to mixed audiences all the time. What binds the audience together is the occasion. Most enter with certain expectations of what they will hear and how it will be said. There is a comfort in knowing what's coming on a given occasion. But there is a difference between comfort and complacency. Complacency is an elbow in the side, nudging you to try an unexpected style.

When you "break the rules," break them intelligently. Have a good reason for adopting a style that at first seems inappropriate. Read your audience well, and they will understand you; read the occasion well, and the audience will embrace you.

Write for captivation

Language that is clear and correct must also captivate the audience. Figures of speech, such as similes and metaphors, are much more than simple aids to clarity. They cast a net around the mind of the audience, holding it captive to the thought you are expressing. The thought has time to work on the person who receives it in the same way that medicine works in the body of a patient who takes it. The well-worded thought is like a timed-release capsule, slowly feeding implications and applications into the lifestream. In this sense, the thought owns the thinker.

Working in concrete images, and archetypal motifs rather than abstract principles will help the congregation see the truth clearly, but it will also create in them a desire to explore that truth more deeply. It's as if you have taken them into Ideas R Us and shown them a shiny new concept they've always wanted. Then you surprise them by letting them take it home and play with it. People cannot explore what they do not own. Captivating language buys the thought and lets the audience take it home. It gives them ownership.

So, the best language works like super strength glue, uniting the concept and the congregation in a permanent bond. The union of thought and thinker is like a good marriage. Unsure of one another at first, they grow to love and live together in harmony. Then, as both mature, they generate action that is consistent with the character of both.

We can reinforce the union of thought and thinker by drafting into service words and sentences that unfurl on the mind with color and dignity. Use gritty nouns, verbs that resonate—words of force. Use short words. Use short sentences. Prune unnecessary words and syllables, but don't strip all the leaves from the tree. We need some verbal foliage for beauty's sake.

What to avoid

We have already hit on a few of the more obvious bumps you want to avoid in manuscripting your sermon. Here are a few potholes to watch for.

Apologies

Good style doesn't need to apologize for itself. "Forgive the personal illustration." That kind of false modesty is self-serving, and it hobbles the illustration. If you need to apologize for an illustration, don't use it.

Introductions

"Allow me to illustrate." "Let me conclude." "Please, allow me to begin by saying, . . ." Don't introduce an illustration, conclusion, or introduction. Simply illustrate, conclude, or begin.

Superlatives

"This is absolutely, positively, the most wonderful message you will ever hear!" Say it well. Say it briefly. Leave them wanting more.

Trite expressions

Find a new way of expressing an old truth. James Kilpatrick says of trite expressions that we need to brush them away since they "fall like casual dandruff on the fabric of our prose."[6]

Good style, like the Christian life, is not something that you "arrive at." It is a growth process that takes time and dedication to the discipline of becoming a forger of ideas.

Words—our tools

Here are some suggestions on how to use words effectively:

Read about style

Kilpatrick, James J. *The Writer's Art*, New York: Andrews, McMeel and Parker, 1984.

Lederer, Richard. *The Miracle of Language*. New York: Simon and Shuster, Pocket Books, 1991.

Nichols, Sue. *Words on Target: For Better Christian Communication*. Louisville: John Knox, 1963.

Strunk, William, Jr., and E. B. White. *The Elements of Style*, 3d ed. New York: Macmillan, 1979.

Zinsser, William. *On Writing Well: An Informal Guide to Writing Nonfiction*, 3d ed. New York: Harper and Row, 1985.

Use good dictionaries and thesauri

Favorite word tools of syndicated columnist James J. Kilpatrick include:[7]

6. James J. Kilpatrick, *The Writer's Art* (New York: Andrews, McMeel and Parker, 1984), 58.

7. Ibid., 141–49. Kilpatrick includes other works he has found deficient for one reason or other. His evaluation of those books makes delightful reading simply for the pleasure of his style. Of Kilpatrick's book, William F. Buckley writes in the foreword, "Not only the best book of its kind I have experienced, . . . it is the most compelling reading about writing that I have ever seen."

The American Heritage Dictionary, 2d College ed. Boston: Houghton Mifflin, 1985.

Webster's Ninth New Collegiate Dictionary. Springfield, Mass.: Merriam-Webster, 1988.

Read classic literature aloud

If you don't know where to begin in your reading, look at:

Fadiman, Clifton. *The Lifetime Reading Plan,* 3d ed. New York: Harper and Row, 1988.

Ryken, Leland. *Realms of Gold.* Wheaton: Ill, Harold Shaw, 1991.

Listen to the media

Radio programs can be particularly helpful. National Public Radio's "Morning Edition" and "All Things Considered" often contain readings from, and interviews with, current authors. Whether you agree with what the authors and commentators have to say, they consistently offer a high quality of writing.

Rewrite to clarify, correct, and captivate

You can almost always improve a sermon by rewriting with a renewed focus on these three important principles.

Speak often

There is no substitute for practice. You can write all week, but until you try it out on people you won't know if it really works.

Revising and repeating sermons

Those who have repeated sermons in Bible conferences or as guest preachers in other churches know the value of preaching the same sermon more than once. Each time try to improve the word choice, the structure, the emphasis, the support materials, and the applications. When you preach the same sermon, you know what works and what needs further development. You need to watch out for an increased confidence level that may entice you to rely more on your own ability than on the Spirit of God to get your points across.

Take a look at the sermon manuscript for Matthew 15 in the appendix. Note the absence of an outline format. The manuscript takes on a mechanical quality when you break it down into points and subpoints. Simply incorporate the statements in the outline into the manuscript without designating them as points. If you wish you may highlight to underscore different outline points, using a "bold" command if working on a computer. This will help you see how much time you are devoting to each major section of the sermon.

The interior of your sermon is complete. You have designed and constructed a message capable of transporting

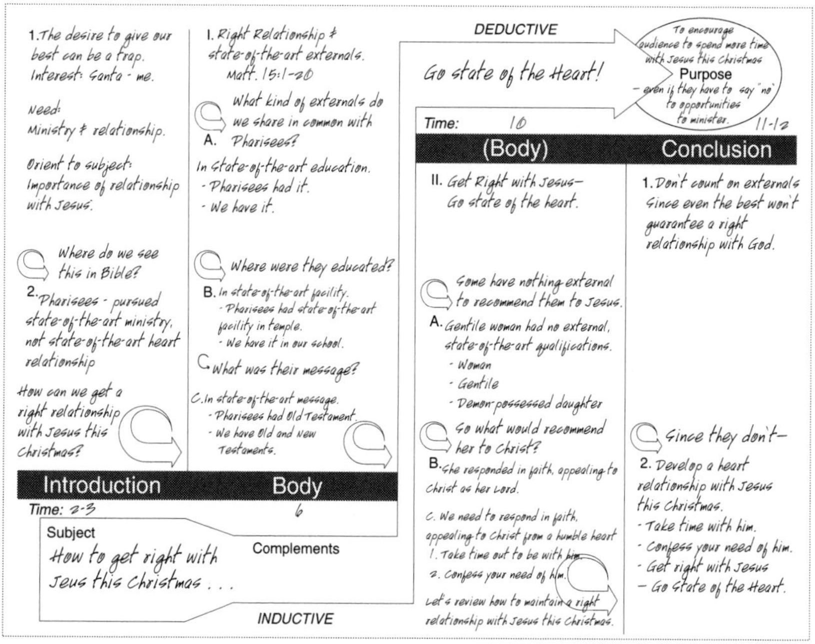

Figure 8.1

Part 4

Charting the Voyage

9

Designing the Flight Plan: Time Lines

How Do I Pace Myself to Arrive on Time?

T minus three.

Maintain your time—sustain their interest.

One of the authors is a retired Air Force Reserve chaplain who served flying units most of his career. The flight plan is the essence of military flying. The first question is always, "Where are you going?" The next questions follow logically: "Why are you going there? What do you plan to do when you arrive?" The entire trip is carefully charted and monitored.

Good sermons should be as well planned and should arrive at their destinations on time. Sadly, this is often not the case. With sermons as with life, the best finish well. What is your on-time arrival percentage? If you were an airline, would people fly with you regularly?

Eudora Welty is the established queen of American
short story writers. She related the nature of her art with
the joy of taking automobile trips with her parents when
she was a child. Usually the trips were to visit her grand-
parents. The trip became to her the communication model
for the stories she wrote.

> The trips were wholes unto themselves. They were stories.
> Not only in form but in their taking on direction, move-
> ment, development, change. They changed something in
> my life: each trip made its particular revelation, though I
> could not have found words for it. . . . When I did begin to
> write, the short story was a shape that had already formed
> itself and stood waiting in the back of my mind.[1]

We share her opinion and have used the metaphor of the
trip throughout this book. This chapter is designed to bring
it all together. For those who can relate to this ideal image
of childhood, a good sermon is like a trip to Grandma's
house. It is filled with visions of the destination. What a joy
to kiss Grandma, to hug Grandpa and to sit down to a mar-
velous meal! What a pleasure to top it off with Grandma's
apple pie and home-made ice cream! Those who enjoyed
such trips can remember the fulfillment of a happy chat
around the table after the meal.

But many of our sermons fail to arrive on time. Some
preachers seem to feel that time is not important. What a
sad thing to plan ahead so poorly that we have to call
Grandma from a wayside phone to tell her we have run out
of time and can't make it today. Or, even worse, we come
screeching to the curb so late that we can only wave to
Grandma as she stands in the doorway, then leave while
the children scream their disapproval in the back seat. A

---

1. Eudora Welty, *One Writer's Beginnings* (Cambridge, Mass.: Harvard University Press, 1984), 68.

sermon that doesn't arrive in time to kiss Grandma and enjoy what she has prepared is a bad sermon.

Many sermons have no flight plan, so they never arrive anywhere. They just run out of time and stop. Some preachers are noted for their tendency to take side excursions. If they ever do arrive at the preplanned destination it's too late for any meaningful spiritual transactions.

Young pastors often have great difficulty getting to the end of the sermon in time to reap the harvest of responses for which they have prayed. They may know where they are going and what to do when they get there. They just can't get everything said they planned to say. One of the greatest problems with preachers is not that they don't know when or how to stop. Rather, they don't know what to leave out so that they can end on time.

Many of you who have read this far are saying, "I don't think I can use the sermon model that is being proposed. I can't get everything on it that I want to say." Perhaps you are putting so much into your sermons that you never get to kiss Grandma.

We have named this book *The Power Sermon* because we believe it will help you arrive at your preaching destination in time to reap responses. Many times we can do more if we try to do less. A carefully developed sermon that is balanced in all its required elements will accomplish more than flooding an audience with information. A sermon that does not arrive at its destination in time to fulfil its purpose is never a satisfactory spiritual experience.

What shall I leave out?

A very accomplished pastor asked for an evaluation of his preaching because, "I'm not sure why, but when I finish my sermon, I am utterly exhausted, and so is my congregation."

After the sermon he was told, "You are a fine preacher. Your problem is quite simple: You had enough content for two sermons. Then you have to rush to get it all said. You are wearing everybody out!"

The question then becomes, "How do I know what to take out and what to leave?"

The answer, "Stick with the essentials!"

If you know what you are talking about (subject), what you are saying about your subject (complement), why you are saying it (purpose), and how long you have to say it, then you can determine what to leave out. Answers to the focusing questions in chapter 3 (see pp. 50–54) are crucial to this process. If after such careful evaluation you still have too much, cut more, make two sermons, or expand it into a series.

There seems to be an inner compulsion by many preachers to preach dump truck sermons. They have to try to say everything they have developed from their exegesis. In topical exposition they have great trouble limiting the sermon subject. The result is often sermon burnout for preacher and people. The urge to be helpful is commendable. The lack of discipline in sermon construction is deplorable.

Let us think through an Easter message that views Christ's passion through the eyes of the Centurion at the cross. The sermon is for an Easter sunrise service and can take no longer than thirty minutes. It seems necessary to gain at least some level of mastery of the events of passion week as recorded in the four Gospels. It is also imperative that the several passages involving the centurion be exegeted. Next the history of the period has to be consulted. What was the Roman army like? Where did they live while in Jerusalem? How did the trials of Christ unfold? How much of the trial did the Centurion witness? Who were the soldiers who guarded Jesus' tomb?

Here is enough material for a sermon six hours long. The first cutting comes as a result of knowing the subject. *The Centurion had witnessed many crucifixions. Jesus was like no other man he had crucified* (subject). The first main point follows: *In contrast to those who struggled to stay alive, Jesus willingly yielded himself to crucifixion.* He died like an innocent Passover lamb. In the words of the Centurion, "Surely this was a righteous man" (Luke 23:47).

To make this first point, we must move through the six stages of Christ's trial, the account of the scourging, and Christ's terrible trip to Golgotha. Obviously much of what you know remains unsaid. But because you know the subject and first complement, you know what must be left out.

The Centurion declared the second way in which the death of Christ differed from the death of all other men was that *Jesus died the way a God would die*: "Surely he was the Son of God" (Matt. 27:54; Mark 15:39). During the entire trial Jesus was the only one composed and in control. At the end he even dismissed his own spirit.

Third, the death of Jesus was like the death of no other man in that *he refused to stay in the tomb*. He rose from the dead. No Roman emperor had ever done that. How would the centurion learn of the resurrection of Christ? Remember that the Jewish priests gave the soldiers guarding the tomb a large sum of money (Matt. 28:12–15). When soldiers have money, they usually drink too much. When soldiers drink, they talk. It could not be far wrong to guess that all the soldiers quartered in Jerusalem were aware of what happened at the tomb of Jesus. You might not want to preach that point, but it seems consistent with the historical setting.

The purpose of the sermon is clear: *to encourage the congregation to worship Christ alone*. By knowing the subject, complements, purpose and time limit you know what to omit.

How long should a sermon be?

It is our observation after years of sermon evaluation that most thirty-five-minute and forty-minute sermons are really thirty-minute sermons with a "wait" problem. They need to lose some verbal fat. Some will argue for a shorter length, and that is fine. Just adjust this discussion to the needs of that time limit. But we must agree at the outset never to waste or misuse the precious time given for the sermon. We live in a media conscious society. Life is ruled by breaks that occur on the hour and the half hour. Television executives plan programs down to the second. We must learn to do the same. Time lines rule television script writers, making them account for every second of a program. Sermon makers ought to become more conscious of time. You can use the sermon model this book proposes to develop time awareness. Here is how a typical thirty-minute sermon might effectively use the given time:

Figure 9.1
30-Minute Sermon
two main points

Introduction	Body		Conclusion
	Point 1	Point 2	
5 Min.	11 Min.	11 Min.	3 Min.

You make your own decisions as to how to use the time available. This linear view of a sermon in relationship to real time can do positive things for your preaching. Remember that these time segments include transitions. Rushing through transitions is like turning corners in your car on two wheels. It puts safe arrival at the destination in serious danger.

Now look at the time constraints of a three-point sermon if all the points are equal in their use of time.

Figure 9.2
30-Minute Sermon
three main points

Introduction	Body			Conclusion
	Point 1	Point 2	Point 3	
5 Min.	7 Min.	7 Min.	7 Min.	4 Min.

We believe that organizing a sermon around more than three points usually makes a sermon into a grocery list. Who wants to spend time remembering grocery lists? It might be better to divide the material into two sermons. In any case, look at the time constraints of a four-point sermon. You will agree that adequately developing six major segments with effective transitions is extremely difficult.

Figure 9.3
30-Minute Sermon
four main points

Introduction	Body				Conclusion
	Point 1	Point 2	Point 3	Point 4	
4 min.	5 min., 30 sec.	5 min., 30 sec.	5 min., 30 sec.	5 min., 30 sec.	4 min.

Sermons do not require points that are equal in time. Some points may be more significant than others. Frederick W. Robertson, a nineteenth-century English preacher, specialized in two point sermons. The first two points in Figure 9.4 came from Robertson's insights. In adapting his splendid sermon on the loneliness of Christ, however, a third point does seem appropriate. Here is a modern adaptation of that sermon, developing three points.

Figure 9.4

30-Minute Sermon
"The Loneliness of Christ,
Revealed in Three Varying Yet Cumulative Degrees"

Introduction	Body			Conclusion
	Point 1	Point 2	Point 3	
Christ was lonely	Isolated in space	Isolated in spirit	Separated from the Father	Christ was lonely in our place.
3 Min.	4 Min.	8 Min.	12 Min.	3 Min.

Christ was often spatially isolated. He was alone. But the Father was with him so this could not be called true loneliness. Christ was also isolated in spirit. Even his closest disciples did not understand the grand purposes that drove him. Yet the Father's presence guided and encouraged him. But in Calvary's divine mystery Christ was for a time separated from the Father. This is the true loneliness of Christ. He bore in his own body the loneliness of separation from God that we all deserve because of our sin. Trust Christ and never be lonely again.

At this point you may be asking, "How can I stay on time?"

Television producers use time cards to let people know how much time remains. In college debate competition time is very important. Time cards keep debate tournaments from extending beyond limits. In preaching classes time cards are extremely useful to show the amount of time left. You might try using time cards or a clock. If you preach on radio or television, you will be cut off if you go overtime. All of us have heard the old joke about the church that installed a trap door behind the pulpit. When the time came for the sermon to be over, the door opened and the preacher disappeared. Have you ever wondered how that joke got started?

Practice makes perfect

To develop a sense of timing commit yourself to the importance of time. The sermon model we propose can be of great help in this regard. You can enhance this discipline by planning to use a certain amount of time for each segment of a sermon. Any preacher can master the use of time. It is like any other discipline: At first it may be difficult, but with practice mastery emerges.

Time difficulties can occur where you do not expect them. One beginning preacher had problems ending his sermons well, so he played his sermon tapes to diagnose the trouble. It turned out he was taking more time than necessary to tell illustrative stories. After concentrated practice on the sermon stories the impact on his preaching was dramatic. The sermon model used in this book allows you to analyze trouble spots. Listen to a tape of your sermon with the model before you. Grade yourself on each area; then develop a plan for improvement. You might plan to work particularly hard on an area until you have adequate control. If you are weak in introductions, work on them until you gain mastery. If you have slighted transitions, spend time mastering that process. If, like most of us, your conclusions are weak, emphasize them until you gain mastery.

What about side trips?

The simple solution to overlong sermons is to use available time carefully. Good sermons, like well-aimed arrows, go directly to their targets. Plan your trip and follow your plan.

Some will say, "I like to give the Holy Spirit opportunity to guide me while I preach. What if I feel led to add something that is not in the plan?"

Surely many genuine works of the Spirit of God have spurred great revivals through such preaching. We would never wish to subdue the work of the Spirit. We do believe, however, that preachers will generally do better to seek the work of the Spirit while in the study preparing.

A simple rule of logic governs sermon digressions. If you add something not on the flight plan you must take something else out. If you do not there is no hope that you will arrive on time.

As a chaplain in the Air National Guard one of the authors preached regularly on the Sundays of monthly drill weekends. The allotted time was thirty-five minutes for the entire service, and the commander required that services *always* end on time. Many times singing groups came on base to bring special music. Since they were willing to come they were usually allowed to sing two numbers. The songs were of varying length. A preacher in such a circumstance quickly becomes expert in taking things out of sermons. It is an art that any pastor can and ought to learn.

Digressions are generally the problem of an undisciplined mind. If you tend to wander while preaching, it might be wise to ask your congregation how they feel about the issue. A candid discussion with your spouse and individual church leaders might be of great help. If you have not regularly sought such feedback, the first responses probably will be cautious. When people discover that you are a serious seeker after truth and will not respond defensively, they will expose their true feelings. Such interaction should not only improve your on-time arrival percentage but other areas of your preaching as well.

Media people have become masters at using time. Those of us who waste time through poor planning need to carefully evaluate our sermons. This is a discipline vital for the effectiveness of pulpit ministry.

Chapter summary:

Time lines

1. Cut out unnecessary verbiage.
2. Leave out details that fail to advance the progress of the message.
3. Assign a certain number of minutes to each major section.
4. Practice!
5. Avoid side trips.

10

Trusting the Inner Compass: Memory

Can I Remember the Way, or Must I Keep Glancing At the Map?

T minus two.

When we focus on memory the issue at stake is interest.

"All of your speeches will be delivered without notes." These were the words of Dr. Paul Carmack. It was a Ph.D.-level public speaking course at Ohio State University. Class members groaned disapproval. How could they survive without notes?

Dr. Carmack's response should be pondered by all who speak in public, particularly by those who preach the Bible. He stated flatly, "If you can't remember what you are going to say long enough to say it, how do you expect anyone to carry it out of the room?"

Students may not use notes when preaching in class at Dallas Theological Seminary. This has always been a major cause of concern among homiletics students. Unfortunately many grab the "Linus blanket" of notes as soon as they leave the classroom.

If you are addicted to notes, what do you do when asked to speak at a banquet. People seated beside you may be in perfect position to read your notes before you do. How do you handle the Memorial Day address at the local cemetery with a side wind of fifteen knots?

This chapter is an invitation to freedom from notes. It is possible to preach without notes every time you preach.

Can the sermon model help?

The sermon model helps the authors. The only way you can know that it will help you is to try using it in the ways we describe. It took years to develop a communications model that would show an entire sermon on one page, revealing forward movement and dynamic progress, primarily in the transitions. Arrows in the model indicate dynamic progress. From the start using the model brought a pleasant surprise. When the sermon structure had been carefully organized around the structure of the sermon model it was possible to visualize the model while in the pulpit. By walking right through the chart it became easier to hit the target with a wallop, on time every time! That's the primary reason we decided to call this book *The Power Sermon*. It has been a freeing experience, and it just does not seem to work as well with the usual sermon outline. Even after going over and over the outline it has been our experience that points will slip away during delivery.

We hope you will have a similar experience of freedom with the chart. Even after preaching for years the model has made preaching easier. We are vitally interested in how the model works for you.

One of the major reasons that using the model contributes to remembering the sermon seems to be focus. When we clearly define the subject, complements, and purpose, answer the focusing questions, and frame the transitions, the sermon tends to remember itself. There is great drawing power to destinations. All of us who enjoy a well-planned trip know how intent we become on "getting there." The sermon model keeps the destination in sharp focus.

Syd Field makes this clear as he discusses the process of writing a screenplay or movie: "Your story *moves forward* from A to Z; from *setup* to *resolution*. Remember the definition of screenplay *structure*: 'a . . . *progression* of *related* incidents, episodes, and events leading to a dramatic resolution.'"[1]

If you don't know where you are going, you will wander aimlessly and waste everyone's time. When you know where you are going, all you have to do is go directly there. A well-defined destination follows a clearly defined route.

Unity, order, progress

Haddon W. Robinson once gave a brilliant lecture on "Unity, Order, and Progress." These principles not only make moving sermons; they also make sermons easy to remember.

Unity

A sermon should develop one idea. A poem, play, or short story succeeds when it communicates one central proposition or theme. Like other fine literature, a memorable sermon focuses thought. Listeners crave this essential unity. They will take that unified message away with them as if it were a priceless gem that has been cut and polished with care. By singlemindedly devoting the sermon to one theme, rather than developing several, the preacher guards unity as the precious diamond it is.

1. Syd Field, *Screenplay: The Foundations of Screenwriting* (New York: Dell, 1979), 56.

Order

There are other natural memory aids. When students complain to us about preaching without notes, we often reply, "If we really wanted to make it hard for you we would make you memorize the text and take your Bible away from you. We are trying, not to make your life hard, but to make your ministry effective. If you are preaching the text, the sermon should flow out of the text in such a logical way that it is unforgettable."

An expository sermon that walks people through the natural flow of the text is as easy to remember as your mother's name. That remains one of the great benefits of exposition. It is all right there before you in the text.

But what if the progressive development of the sermon is somewhat different from the way the text is laid out? There are many natural aids to memory. We will discuss them more fully in chapter eleven. However, anyone who has had a sermon "click into place" knows its profound effect on memory. A question naturally deserves an answer. A problem demands a solution. A story often follows a sequential path. A proposition begs for an application.

Let us consider a sermon on Hebrews 12:3–13. After exegesis we feel we adequately understand the passage in its context, but a clear sermon does not emerge. Running mentally through the list of natural structures ideas you suddenly remember a model that runs *"symptom, diagnosis, disease, remedy."*

How natural. The sermon snaps into place. You couldn't forget it if you tried. In Hebrews 12:1–2 the writer sets forth principles for running the race of life in gold medal style. Beginning in verse 3, problems have developed. Some were in danger of growing weary and losing heart. Verse 4 indicates that some had grown soft in their attitude toward sin. Verses 5 and 6 reveal negative attitudes towards God's clear instruction in Scripture. Verse 12 discloses that the would-be champions for God had weak hands and feeble knees. Verse thirteen shows them wandering all over the race course rather than going straight for the goal.

These people were not running in gold medal style. They had symptoms of spiritual sickness. Unless the people made major adjustments quickly the result would be tragedy rather than triumph.

The writer of Hebrews makes his diagnosis in verses 5 and 6. The people were despising God's work of discipline. They were in danger of becoming bitter, as the author describes in verses 14 through 17. God's discipline program prods every aspect of human life. It calls for training and correction. But, more than anything, it expresses God's love. God shows that he truly cares by exercising his loving discipline.

I understand the *symptoms*, the *diagnosis*, and the *disease*. What is the *remedy*? In verses 7 through 11 the writer of Hebrews shows his readers that if they will submit to God's loving discipline, they can know they are God's children and experience life from God. Verse 9 fairly shouts: "Submit and live!"

Applications leap from the text. How many medical bills could we avoid by submitting to God? How many failing marriages would be saved if we would only submit to God? How many churches would radiate the power to change lives if we would but submit to God?

Who could forget such a message? The introduction exposes the symptoms, relating them to similar problems we face in our lives today. Next comes a careful analysis of why the symptoms had developed. The key to diagnosis followed naturally. What could be more natural than the presentation of the remedy and a word of hope for those who use it?

Progress

Grady Davis, one of the most influential homileticians of this century, stated, "The proper design of a sermon is a movement in time. It begins at a given moment, it ends at a given moment, and it moves through the intervening moments one after another."[2] That is another way to state the trip metaphor. Movements in time in sequence are easy to remember by following the natural order of the ideas you seek to communicate. You will enhance memory greatly when you plan your sermon trip well and follow your plan. Disjointed, unorganized discourse is very difficult to remember.

Speak extemporaneously

Anyone who has competed in forensic speaking contests knows the difference between impromptu and extemporaneous speeches. Impromptu speakers are given a subject. They must stand up at that moment and deliver a speech. Extemporaneous speakers are given a topic and are allowed a predetermined time to prepare. We do not recommend preaching impromptu sermons.

Extemporaneous preaching means speaking without notes, not without thorough preparation. It becomes possible after a well developed outline has been crafted into a full manuscript. Writing out the sermon allows you to think the thoughts all the way through to their destination. Don't memorize the words. If you are capable of writing it you can say it before an audience. Don't worry about finding those particular words in your memory bank. The act of writing it down serves as a prod to the memory. You will probably find as we have that you will remember naturally those key words and phrases which are most memorable. Those you fail to remember probably weren't necessary anyway.

2. Henry Grady Davis, *Design for Preaching* (Philadelphia: Fortress, 1958), 163–64.

You internalize, rethink and re-experience the sermon as you deliver it to the congregation. You adapt the words of the sermon to the response of the listeners as you speak it. This follows the pattern of normal conversational speech. To make these adaptations the preacher must look into the eyes of the audience. Notes are like chains that hinder this dynamic process. If you fear seeing too much negative response and becoming unsettled, look for the friendly faces. After a time you will become comfortable with such direct involvement. Most people who appear to be unfriendly probably have indigestion.

There is a difference between memorizing a sermon manuscript and mastering a sermon structure. It should help you to place the structure of the sermon on the sermon model we have supplied. Master the transitions. We designed the sermon model so that you can see the entire sermon on a single sheet. The emphasis is on knowing what you are talking about (subject), what you are saying about your subject (complements), why you are saying it (purpose), and how much time you have to say it (time line). The key to preaching without notes is to master these relationships.

Speak from experience

Suppose someone asked you to give a short speech on the major influences your father has had on your life. Most of you could design a speech and deliver it without notes. How is this possible? Those experiences out of your past are vivid in your memory. You have mastery of them. If you work toward this kind of mastery of your sermons you will find that it is possible.

Those of us who have taught public speaking and preaching have experienced a common phenomenon. A student is stumbling through a beginning sermon. He is halting in speech, spasmodic, poker faced, wooden in movement. Suddenly he comes to life. His gestures smooth out. His face becomes alive. The monotone voice takes on a resonant musical tone. For a short time he is transformed into a relaxed, radiant, dynamic preacher. What happened? The student gave an illustration out of personal experience.

Think through what took place. Notice that there was no problem with memory. Why was that? Primarily because there was a high degree of personal mastery. Power, freedom, and control flowed from that mastery. People who must preach in English as a second language often have great fear of speaking without notes. It helps them and those who listen to them if they use illustrations out of their culture and experience.

Now analyze the experience again. What makes the telling of personal life experiences a more positive event? Do you notice how the relating of the event was merely the re-telling of a story composed of a series of images? The video recorder of your mind replayed the images and you related them. As you are learning to preach without notes you might start with a vivid personal memory. Next, experiment with an illustration from another source. Run the video camera of your mind over the scene a few times. Master the sequences of the account. Soon you will be able to stand and tell the illustration with the same freedom you have as you relate your own experience.

Perhaps this video camera effect of the mind explains why some of us more easily remember a sermon placed on the power sermon model. It may fit more readily into our sensory equipment than does a traditional outline. The imagery of the model seems to anchor thoughts to the mind in a way that a traditional outline does not.

In chapter 11 we will review a number of sermon strategies. Many of these use progressive images that are easy to remember. Building a structure for the sermon that is full of images can be a great aid to the memory. Some of us find sermons based on biblical narrative simple to remember because of the clear story line. The New Testament writers were masters of memorable images. We should learn from them.

When the apostle Paul discussed the ministry of reconciliation in 2 Corinthians 5:11–21, he made ample use of the term *ambassador*. The images that surround the office of ambassador are rich in most countries of the world. Paul then states vividly that he and Timothy are fellow workers with the Corinthian church. *Fellow workers* emits positive images. After discussing his extreme hardships, he says his heart is open to them and he wishes they would open up their hearts to him (6:11–12). Paul then encourages them, through a series of picturesque contrasts, to avoid being unequally yoked to unbelievers (6:14–7:1).

Try using images like those of Paul in your sermons. Relate your proposition to images. Review chapter 8 and notice how style can be an aid to memory (pp. 132–38). Learn to think in pictures and notice how your memory improves.

Avoid clutter

A very positive aid to memory is simplicity. Chapter 9 discussed the difficulty of arriving at the end of a sermon on time if you load too much into the outline (pp. 149–52). Consider the same argument regarding memory. The fewer the points, the less you have to remember. Two points are easier to remember than six points. Two or three clear pictures provide the mind with better hooks to hang the sermon on than a photo album full of poorly focused snapshots. The more vivid and concrete the images the easier the thoughts to remember. Try to do more by doing less. Do it with more vivid imagery and notice how your memory leaps in ability. You will probably also notice a marked improvement in the attentiveness of your audience.

If you add something to the sermon that is too complex to remember be assured that the congregation will not remember it. Why not have it printed as part of the church bulletin or make it available for interested people?

Above all, avoid grocery or laundry list points. If you are a devotee of minutiae this may be a challenge. Pray and search until you find a way to group concepts under major headings. Pepper shot lacks punch. It rarely brings home the bacon.

Rehearse, rehearse, rehearse

The move to Dallas, Texas, from Cedarville, Ohio, was a change from village life to metropolitan living for one of the authors and his family. The drive to Dallas Seminary was like threading through a maze. But after just a few trips there was no longer a need for the directions scratched on paper. Finally it was possible to choose from among alternate routes that would take approximately the same time.

Mastering sermon movement is much like that. The first time through can be very tentative. But run over the route a few times and things smooth out. What a good feeling it is to have it down!

There is one great hazard to rehearsing: You have to have something to rehearse. At Dallas Seminary we require students to report by noon of the day before they preach that they have completed the process. Who wants to listen to a sermon preached by a person that has been up all night hammering together the loose ends? For the sake of all who listen to you, finish in time to run some solid rehearsals. The self-imposed deadline that assures adequate rehearsal will surely produce better sermons.

Concentrate, concentrate, concentrate

Perhaps the single greatest aid to memory is concentration. After completing high school, the U.S. Army Medical Corps, college, and seminary, one of the authors realized that God's plan for his life required a Ph.D. While pastoring full time and teaching public school part-time he worked toward a master of arts degree at a state university to earn the right to go on. There was no time to waste, and he discovered ways to make better use of class time. Sitting at the front of the room cut out distractions. Taking copious notes forced him to listen carefully.

Learning to concentrate was hard going at first. But soon the class periods seemed to be only five minutes long. Even the most boring professor had profound things to say for those who listened. Exams became a cake walk. After concentrated listening a brief review got the job done. Better concentration also began to affect his preaching. By concentrating during preparation he could get the sermon notes solidly in mind. He still carried notes into the pulpit. Just in case. But then came the realization that he had not looked at a note in weeks. Why not be free? From then on the notes were left in the office.

That liberation can happen to any preacher willing to pay the price of concentration. We live in the midst of a clanging cacophony of distractions. Concentration is the discipline of mind that shuts them out and dwells on the project at hand. Preachers who do first-person narrative dramatic sermons in costume know that when you step out to do a Bible character concentration is the order of the day. There is no pulpit for notes, no prompter but the Spirit of God. What challenge! What freedom!

Go ahead—Jump in!

Everything has to start somewhere. Leaders must feel free to fail. Trust your memory. Start with personal experience illustrations. Enjoy the exhilaration of success. Then try to remember other illustrations. Wean yourself away from your notes.

If you forget a part of your sermon, who will know but you? The people would probably have forgotten it as soon as you said it anyway. It is really encouraging when you stop to think about it: What you forget is probably eminently forgettable. What you remember will be more memorable for others as well, and that's cause for rejoicing.

Trust your memory. Better yet, trust the Lord, whose memory never fails, to help you remember those things he wants his people to hear. It is amazing what you can remember when you relax, concentrate, and trust in him for your success. But how will you ever know until you try?

Chapter summary:

Memory

1. Know your destination.
2. Maintain unity, order, and progress in getting there.
3. Speak extemporaneously.
4. Speak from experience.
5. Avoid clutter.
6. Rehearse.
7. Concentrate.

11

Taking a Different Route: Creativity in Sermon Structure

Do I Have to Go the Same Way Every Time?

T minus 1.

When we explore different sermon structures we focus on clarity and interest.

Have you ever listened to a preacher who would not let you think about anything else but his sermon? We have. Chuck Swindoll is like that. Just try to force yourself to think about something else while he is preaching. He grabs your mind right back. Would you like to hold attention that way? Such ability is the combination of many factors. Some are part of the preacher's personality. Chuck reads widely and prepares well. His forceful style commands attention. He crafts his messages well and delivers them with enthusiasm. He uses concrete images with effective variety and pacing.

Have you tried to listen to a preacher who could not hold your attention? How long can you force yourself to listen before you begin dozing off or start gathering wool? If you could have put a stop watch on your attention span, you might have been surprised to learn that your attention began to fade after only about twenty or thirty seconds. Comparing that to reading you might have had trouble getting to this sentence if you started at the beginning of the chapter. That's the way we are. Could it be one of the weaknesses of human life that came from the fall of our first parents in Eden? It is a chronic problem for all of us.

The producers of television programs and movies are well aware of this difficulty. They work very hard to make their programs and films compelling. Boring movies don't earn good ratings. Tedious television shows are turned off. Humdrum sermons face a similar fate. The preacher who preaches monotonous sermons is tuned out by the congregation long before being turned out of the parsonage.

What can we do? We can learn some valuable lessons from the media attention-getters.

Dr. Harrison B. Summers taught radio and television broadcasting at Ohio State University. Born around the turn of this century, he watched with rapt fascination the development of motion pictures, radio, and television. He served on the Federal Communication Commission for several years. Few people have gained mastery of media at his level, and much of this chapter is adapted from Dr. Summers' strong emphasis on holding attention during broadcast programs. A foremost principle is that to hold attention *we must give the listener something new at frequent intervals*. When we offer something new we regain audience attention.

Milo O. Frank agrees that the attention span of the average person is about thirty seconds. He suggests a simple experiment: Concentrate on a lamp. Your mind will move to some other thought within thirty seconds. He observes,

"If the lamp could move or talk, or go on or off by itself, it would capture your attention for another 30 seconds. But without motion or change, it cannot hold you."[1]

Try viewing a prime time television program with a stop watch in hand. Write down the number of seconds that pass before there is a change of some kind. Even on a talk show, action or subject is changed frequently. Some talk show hosts interrupt if a speaker takes too long to make a point. The average length of the units or segments ranges from about thirty seconds to two minutes. The so-called "sound bite" news segment is usually about thirty seconds long. It may be preceded by a thirty-second setup and followed by a thirty-second summary. Commercials are usually no longer than thirty seconds.

We must regularly give the congregation something new or different to hold their attention. If people are not listening, why speak?

Providing this variety is not really as hard as it sounds. Below is a list of elements or units available for use in a sermon. You can probably think of others. Remember that everything you say in a sermon takes time. Time is directly related to interest. All elements must have vivid wording and be delivered with vocal and physical energy to enhance interest. No element, with the possible exception of a graphic story, should ever last more than two minutes without a significant change.

Some of the sermon elements available for use include:

- reading or quoting Scripture text or texts
- statement of proposition, main points, or subpoints.
- restatement of points
- repetition
- transitional statements

1. Milo O. Frank, *How To Get Your Point Across In Thirty Seconds Or Less* (New York: Pocket Books, 1986), 15.

- description or narration of text or contextual details
- grammatical detail
- definition
- exhortation
- application
- argumentation, reasoning, proof
- quotation or testimony
- figures of speech[2]
- questions, interrogation
- illustration or example: Specific instances, real or hypothetical; anecdotes; human interest accounts; stories; parables; fables, or analogies. Illustrations must include graphic word pictures of how persons, animals, or things look, feel, and act.
- humorous incidents, jokes
- statistics
- object lessons
- visual aids: film clips; slides; charts; or overhead transparencies
- dramatic vignettes
- poetry
- songs
- instrumental interludes (musical bridging)
- handouts of printed material

It should be clear that preachers can choose from a varied menu. But people are so easily distracted. If we do not put our sermons together effectively we will lose interest, even while speaking with variety. People will not work to listen, particularly the people you want most to reach. Enhance ease of listening by using "The Seven Laws of Effective Broadcasting." These are structural requirements that govern television and radio programing. Writers for broad-

2. See E. W. Bullinger, *Figures of Speech Used in the Bible* (Grand Rapids: Baker, 1968).

cast must comply with these seven structural requirements. Success demands all seven in every program:

1. program unity—one and only one idea
2. effective opening and closing
3. strong start—Grab interest or lose the viewer
4. variety in materials used
5. unit-to-unit contrast and change
6. good pacing—the effect of moving
7. effective building to a climax

The well-structured broadcast program, whether on radio or television, must satisfy these requirements. These seven demands also rest upon the sermon that would touch hearts and move people to action. If media producers work hard to create dynamic programing, dare we do less in preaching God's truth?

Sermons that sizzle

Ask yourself the following questions about every sermon you preach:

Unity: Am I preaching one central proposition and only one? Do all parts of my sermon carry forward my central proposition?

Opening and closing: Does my sermon have an effective introduction and conclusion?

Strong start: Do I get down to business?

Variety: Is my sermon a drab flatland or a rolling panorama of mountains and valleys, streams, rivers, and lakes? Have I used a wide variety of sermon elements?

Unit-to-unit contrast and change: Have I included contrast and change in sermon elements? Is any element too long to hold interest? Have I been careful not to sacrifice unity as I sought change?

Effective pace: Does my sermon move forward to its destination? Does everything in the sermon move it forward to the goal? Have I bogged down in some exegetical marsh just because the details interest me? Do I speak with a wide variety of rate, volume, and pitch?

Building to a climax: Have I saved the best to last or will I run out of time and stop short of my goal? Where is the ebb and flow? Is there a strong sense of building to climax? Have I piled so much on my sermon wagon that I will break its axle?

Remember: Every sermon must demonstrate all seven structural requirements to hold interest to the end. Evaluate Christ's Sermon on the Mount using the criteria listed above. Jesus gets high marks in all categories. Try reading the sermon aloud. Notice how quickly Jesus introduced something new. Jesus made us. He knows how we work. We can learn from him.

Variety in sermon form

The structure of the text normally forms the shape of the sermon. But the needs of the people and the purpose of the sermon often require a sermon strategy slightly different from this flow. As noted in chapters 1 and 2, the sermon still must remain consistent with what is taught in its Scripture context.

Haddon W. Robinson describes the basic shapes sermons take in chapter eight of *Biblical Preaching*.[3] You could profit from a review of that chapter. We have provided examples of the power sermon model for sermons that are *deductive, inductive,* and *inductive-deductive combinations.* Let's see how these forms relate to the model.

3. Haddon W. Robinson, *Biblical Preaching* (Grand Rapids: Baker, 1980), 114–34.

Deductive sermon structure

Deductive structures have been popular with many preachers over the years. Some of us are familiar with the following advice:

Tell them what you are going to tell them.
Tell them.
Tell them what you told them.

Present the central proposition in the introduction. The main points then develop the points of the sermon. If deductive sermons pass the test of the seven requirements of effective program structure they also can be very interesting. Deductive sermons can present essential truths with great clarity. The following sermon on the demands of true discipleship can have powerful effect.

Introduction
   1.
   2.
   3. Central Proposition: *True discipleship demands undivided loyalty, unselfish devotion, and unquestioning service.*
  I. True discipleship demands *undivided loyalty.*
     A. You have to reject family ties.
     B. Family ties drag you down.
     C. Give your undivided loyalty to Jesus Christ.
  II. True discipleship demands *unselfish devotion.*
     A. You have to reject personal rights.
     B. Personal rights draw you away.
     C. Give your unselfish devotion to Jesus Christ.
  III. True discipleship demands *unquestioning service.*
     A. You have to reject reasonable choices.
     B. Reasonable choices direct you out of God's will.
     C. Give your unquestioning service to Jesus Christ.
Conclusion

On the deductive sermon model this might be set up as in Figure 11.1.

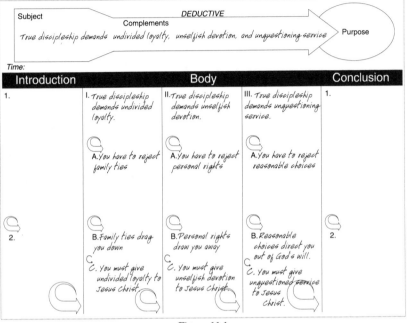

Figure 11.1

In recent years inductive sermon development has garnered much attention. Some have criticized deductive development because contemporary audiences seem to prefer to have ideas held in tension throughout the sermon. While this may be true in many cases, the day of effective deductive preaching is far from over. The major concern must always be to find the best way to handle a particular text or topic for a specific audience. You can develop some sermons deductively or inductively or with a combination of the forms. Sometimes it is helpful to read the scripture passage deductively. To do this you would state the proposition of the passage before your oral reading of the text. You can reflect your emphasis in the way you read.

Inductive sermon structure

Inductive development can produce creative tension that makes sermons more interesting. Inductive sermons, handled improperly, can also lead to utter confusion. You must treat introductions and transitions with great care when you attempt inductive development. Orientation to the subject in the introduction keeps the audience from wondering what you are talking about. Careful structuring of transitions reminds the audience that you are still talking about the same thing. If people don't know what you are talking about, they will usually think about something else.

Inductive sermons differ from deductive structure in that you do not present the full proposition of the inductive sermon until the end. This is the natural structure of stories. Everyone knows what happens when the punch line of a joke pops out before the teller is ready for it. Often inductive sermons are first-person narratives. In these sermons some orientation to the subject must be presented in the introduction, but the proposition does not develop until the end. For example, in a narrative sermon from the prophet Hosea, the structure of the sermon follows the unfolding of the story. At the very end of the sermon Hosea says . . .

> I have come to know in the depth of my being how desperately God loves sinners, how deliberately he seeks them, with what devotion he woos them to himself.

And in a narrative sermon on Genesis 22, concerning Abraham's willingness to offer his son Isaac, Abraham concludes with a statement to Sarah:

> We never need fear to go to the place of God's plan for it will be the place of God's provision.

With inductive sermon structure the reading of the text can be delayed until adequate tension has been developed. By that time the audience should have some questions that the text can answer. If you read the Scripture well, the proposition, which is the answer to the question, should pop into the minds of the listeners.

Most concerns related to preaching inductive sermons can be answered best under the discussion of the inductive-deductive form.

Inductive-deductive structure

This sermon form involves clear orientation to the subject in the introduction. Transitions keep the subject clear. Emphasis is on the development of interest through tension or anticipation of an outcome. Notice how our now familiar "State of the Heart" sermon develops:

Introduction
  1. Interest: Becoming Santa Clause for my kids illustrates the fate of most dads who want to give the best to their families at Christmas.
  2. Need: The desire to give our best can subtly trap us into substituting ministry for relationship.
  3. Orientation to subject: We need to be careful to maintain a right relationship with Jesus this Christmas.
  4. Orientation to text: The Pharisees substituted ministry for relationship when they relied on their "state of the art" training to qualify them before the Lord.
  5. Structural Overview: This morning we will consider one way to maintain a right relationship with Jesus this Christmas.

Body
  I. You aren't guaranteed a right relationship with God through state of the art externals (Matt. 15:1–20).
     A. You aren't guaranteed a right relationship with God through state of the art education.

      1. The Pharisees had a state of the art education.

      2. We have a state of the art education.

   B. You aren't guaranteed a right relationship with God in a state of the art facility.

      1. The Pharisees had a state of the art facility.

      2. We have a state of the art facility.

   C. You aren't guaranteed a right relationship with God if you have a state of the art message.

      1. The Pharisees had a state of the art message.

      2. We have a state of the art message.

II. Get right with Jesus. Go state of the heart (Matt. 15:21–28).

   A. The Gentile woman could appeal to no state of the art qualifications to recommend her to Jesus (vv. 15:21–24).

      1. Her sex, her heritage, and her problem all worked against her (vv. 21–22).

         a. She was a woman, and women were chattel.

         b. She was from Tyre and Sidon, the home town of Jezebel and idolatrous worship.

         c. She had a demon-possessed daughter; children were lower than women on the social ladder.

      2. Her manipulative appeal to Jesus as Jewish Messiah worked against her (vv. 23–24).

   B. Her only hope was to appeal to Christ as her Lord (vv. 25–28).

      1. Her appeal to Jesus as her Lord elicited his response (vv. 25–27).

         a. She acknowledged whom he was in bowing down to worship (v. 25).

         b. She acknowledged whom she was in her humble response to Jesus' observation (vv. 26–27).

      2. Jesus rewarded her humble faith (v. 28).

   C. God readily extends his grace to anyone who bows before him with a humble heart.

      1. A right relationship with God begins with a vision of who God really is.

      2. A vision of who God is will be followed by a humble acknowledgment of our need.

  3. Once we sense our need of him we must take time out
     this busy Christmas season to be alone with the Lord.
  4. Confess your desperate need of him with a humble heart.

Conclusion
  1. State of the art externals do not guarantee a right rela-
     tionship with God.
  2. We will get right with God when we see him for who he
     is and bow our hearts before him in humble dependence.
  3. Quote: "Remember, we do not worship the service of our
     Lord; we worship the Lord of our service."
  4. Take time out this Christmas to get right with God by
     bowing before him alone and worshiping him in the qui-
     etness of your heart.
  5. Get right with Jesus — Go state of the heart.

Eugene L. Lowry has made a significant contribution to
this inductive-deductive form of preaching in *The Homiletical Plot*.[4] He points out that, to maintain high levels of
interest, sermons should develop along the line of narrative art forms. He prefers the word *sequence* to *structure*
and proposes five sequential stages to a typical sermonic
plot. He visualizes the plot as in Figure 11.2.

As in the sermon model with the arrow and the target,
there is strong forward movement. To begin to understand
the plot line, follow the five numbers in sequence:

  1. A *discrepancy* upsets the equilibrium.
  2. There is an *analysis* of the discrepancy.
  3. A *clue* to resolving the discrepancy is presented.
  4. We *experience* resolution through the gospel.
  5. We live in *anticipation* of the consequences.

  4. Eugene L. Lowry, *The Homiletical Plot: The Sermon as Narrative Art Form*
(Atlanta: John Knox, 1980), 24–25. The diagram is used by permission.

Figure 11.2

The Lowry Plot Line

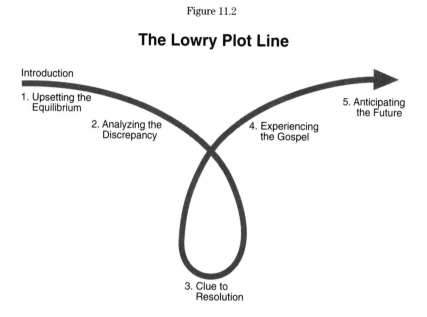

We can illustrate Lowry's stages with a story. Tony becomes ill (1. on Lowry's chart). His equilibrium is definitely
upset. His doctor goes into action to analyze the discrepancy—Tony's symptoms—with examinations, tests, and con-
sultation with other doctors (2. on the chart). Tony, his
parents, and friends wait for the doctor's decision (Lowry
wisely points out that this is the most interesting part of
the process.). Finally a clue to diagnosis (3.) is uncovered.
Everything hinges on this insight or discovery. There is a
reversal. Things start in a new direction. The doctor pre-
scribes the remedy (4.). Tony begins to take the medicine
(Here the preacher applies the Word of God to the problem
or discrepancy.). Tony begins to improve in response to
the treatment (5.). He can now anticipate leaving the hos-
pital and returning to normal life.

The first three phases of Lowry's sermonic plot are inductive in nature. The final two are usually deductive. Nor-

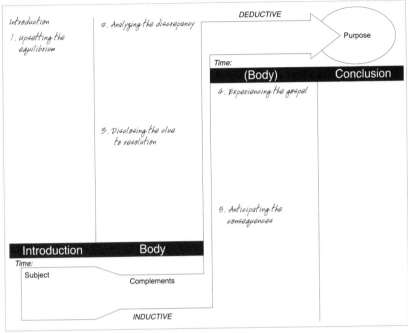

Figure 11.3

mally the preacher would present stage one in the introduction. A suggested application of Lowry's five stages to the power sermon model is found in Figure 11.3.

This formula provides a natural model for Paul's argument in Ephesians 2:1–10. We see the discrepancy in verse 1: Without Christ all people are dead in sin. The discrepancy is analyzed in verses 2a and 3: Human beings can't change their lostness. Now comes the reversal or the key to resolution in the beginning of verse 4: "But God," by love and mercy, provided a way out through Christ. Paul applies the gospel in verses 4–8: What people cannot do for themselves God makes possible by his grace. Verse 10 anticipates the consequences: A new life of service for God.

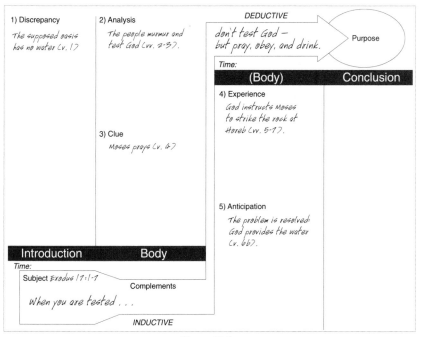

Figure 11.4

While not all biblical texts fit so smoothly into Lowry's diagram, his insight is helpful. Developing sermons in this way can help to keep people involved. When audience members listen to truth, lives are changed.

Figure 11.4 is a sermon from Exodus 17:1–7. The passage relates the account of Moses smiting the rock at Horeb.

You can make many other uses of Lowry's model. Try some creative trips with this method. Remember that variety keeps attention. Why preach if no one is listening? God made you creative. Prayer should not only be the problem solver for Moses but for us as well. He can help you be interesting as you work hard and trust him.

Chapter summary:

Creativity in structure

1. Make sure a sermon contains "The Seven Laws of Effective Broadcasting."
2. Vary sermon structure to meet the need of the audience.
3. For variety construct a sermon adapting Lowry's plot line to the power sermon model.

Appendix A

Sermon Manuscript: "Go State of the Heart" (Matthew 15:1–28)

I invite you to open your Bibles to Matthew, chapter 15.

I stand before you this morning in what Donald Guthrie called the third stage of a man's life. The three stages of a man's life are: He believes in Santa Claus; he does not believe in Santa Claus; he *is* Santa Claus. I love to give presents to my kids at Christmas time . . . anytime really, but especially at Christmas. It just happens when you love someone. And the more deeply you love, the more you want the gift to be—*state of the art*. We all have someone—a mom, a dad, a husband, a wife, or kids. And I've noticed something interesting: What's true on a human-to-human level is also true on a human-to-God level.

If you're in love with Jesus Christ then you want to give him only the best—state of the art. And we usually express our best for him in terms of our ministry for him. That's why you're here, because you are preparing to give to him the best years of your life in full-time service.

But there's danger here, an evil that is sitting—waiting in the shadows of your desire to serve Jesus with the best. This evil is dressed in the servant's towel and carries a basin to wash the feet of the world. The problem is that the towel is monogrammed with your initials, and the bowl is golden, and the soap is perfumed . . . all state of the art.

This slick servant seduces you slowly and, at least at Dallas Seminary, by "degree," and you find yourself falling in love with service and out of love with the One you serve. The Pharisees had been seduced by state-of-the-art service. Their service wasn't an expression of a grateful heart. It was an expression of a guilty heart. A guilty conscience made them want to get right with God, so the Pharisees turned their state-of-the-art service into a bargaining chip designed to make God grateful to *them*. They wanted to get right with God, and service was the way. But they found out what any teenager could have told them—The kind of service that tries to earn love will, in the end, only impress itself. Gradually, they forgot the one they were serving and began to worship the service itself. Not only had they fallen out of love with God, they didn't even recognize him when he walked among them. Please listen as I read verses 1–20.

(Read Matt. 15:1–20)

Jesus is teaching that you aren't guaranteed a right relationship with God through state of the art externals. We in this chapel share some sobering similarities with those Pharisees. Their state-of-the-art service to God comprised at least three elements:

They had a state of the art education. There are people around the world who would give the right side of their brain to be sitting where you are sitting. Some of you have already made that sacrifice, I know.
They had a state of the art facility in the temple. Dallas Seminary has one of the most envied facilities of any seminary in the world.

A state of the art education, and all of that because they
had a state of the art message.

They had the only true God and the only true message
about that God. And they had had that message for a long
time. And we share this in common with them, I think. We
have held our New Testament message for almost as long
as the Pharisees had held their Old Testament message before Jesus came—long enough to develop some self-serving traditions . . . long enough for the traditions to become
the message . . . long enough for external ritual to replace
internal righteousness. See, the Pharisees had backed up
the dump trucks and unloaded all of this traditional sand
on the bedrock truth of God. Over the years they had erect-
ed a monolithic system of works, ostensibly to please God
but really to please people. There it stood, glittering in the
sunlight, the Pharisees gawking at it in all their pride. Jesus
walks up, takes a look, and says, "Hey, that's nothing but a
sand castle." And he turns around and walks away.

There's a spiritual devolution that can take place when
you come to Dallas Seminary if you aren't careful. And it's
so subtle I want to warn you now so you can guard against
it. Do you love the ministry? If the answer is "Yes," then
you may be in danger. "The ministry," whatever that may
mean for you, is not now—nor was it ever intended to be—
an end in itself. The ministry is not now—nor was it ever
intended to be—the object of your affection. When it
comes to getting right with God, all the externals, the state
of the art education, state-of-the-art facilities, and a state
of the art message are nonissues if they replace him as the
object of our affection.

For the Pharisees who possessed so much, it was too
late. But for those whom the Pharisees despised, the door
of heaven was swinging open.

Jesus turns his back on the Pharisees and walks out of
Palestine, the only recorded departure from Palestine in

the Gospels, to go to the district of Tyre and Sidon. And
there he meets (Heavens!) a Canaanite woman. This lady
could appeal to no state of the art qualifications to recommend her to Jesus. Her sex, her heritage, and her problems
all worked against her.

She was a woman, and women were chattel.
She was from Tyre and Sidon, the home town of Jezebel
    and idolatrous worship.
She had a demon-possessed daughter; children were
    lower than women on the social ladder. There was
    nothing lower than a child in the homes of the ancient
    Near East—well, nothing except maybe the house-
    hold pet, the dog that ran around licking crumbs up
    off the floor.

She has absolutely nothing going for her—no social connections, no religious affiliations, no family ties. And she
comes looking for Santa Claus.

(Read Matthew 15:21–28)

Just contrast Jesus' response to the Pharisees and his
response to this lady. It's the difference between condem-
nation and blessing, between heaven and hell. He's teaching us one simple thing, folks: *If you want to get right with
Jesus, go state of the heart.*

Now this Canaanite woman doesn't start out that well.
She has something to learn herself. Perhaps she thought,
"Maybe just a touch of flattery will work," so she appeals
to him by his Davidic title (read v. 22). See, she addressed
him as "Son of David," the Jewish Messiah, and he responded as the Son of David, the Jewish Messiah: "I was
sent only to the lost sheep of the house of Israel."

And then something must have clicked in her Canaanite
mind. "Oh," she said to herself, "I see. I am a Gentile; he is
a Jew. What's more—he is the Messiah to the Jews. Well, if
I can't appeal to him as the Jewish Messiah, I can at least

appeal to him as my master." Verse 25 (Read v. 25). Now things begin to get interesting. Jesus addresses her for the first time. He says, "It isn't good to take this porterhouse steak I've cooked for my Jewish children and serve it to Gentile dogs." She says in verse 27, Yes, Lord; but even the dogs feed on the crumbs that fall from the (what?) their *master's* table."

No more flattery—just an honest recognition of who Jesus is and who she is, and a right response based on that knowledge. Isn't this amazing? Jesus spends most of his time trying to get the Jews to see him for who he is to them while, over here in Gentile territory, he is busy getting this dear lady to see him for who he is to the Gentiles. The Jewish leaders didn't see him for who he was at all. And the Gentile woman didn't see him at first for who he was to the Gentiles.

But here's the big difference. The Jewish leaders didn't need any help. They didn't need a Savior. They didn't even need a Santa Claus, because their ministry was "state of the art," don't you see. But this Gentile woman was desperate for help. They were self-sufficient; she was insufficient. They had state of the art education and facilities; she had none of that—only a humble heart that acknowledged Jesus as her master.

The Pharisees standing proudly contrast with this Canaanite on her knees to teach us a valuable lesson this Christmas, and that lesson is this: Our state of the art service for Christ doesn't guarantee a right relationship with Christ. In fact, that state of the art service can become an idol if we make it an end in itself as the Pharisees did. Are you caught up in the pursuit of state of the art ministry? Pursue Christ instead.

Take some time out this Christmas to get alone with your Lord. Say "no" to some good things so you can say "yes" to the best thing—worshiping him one-on-one. You can graduate from this place with a degree in "Marthaology" and forget that it was Mary who had chosen the better part. Get alone with him. Take some walks, just you and the Lord. Tell him he is your love. Tell him he is your passion, and he will give you the desire of your heart—He will give you himself.

This Christmas, we look to the Canaanite; we don't come to worship the service of our Lord—We come to worship the Lord of our service.

Get right with Jesus this Christmas—Go state of the heart.

Appendix B

Power Sermon Models

The master forms on the following pages may be reproduced for use in working out the various forms of the Power Sermon Model. For best results enlarge them to fit an
eight and one-half inch by eleven inch sheet or larger. Early drafts can be roughed out on hand-sketched models. Included, in order, are forms for deductive, inductive, and
inductive-deductive sermons, and for sermons using the
Lowry Plot Line model.

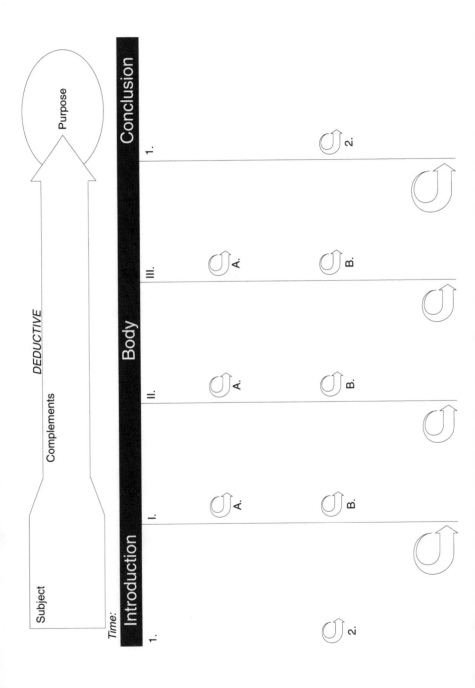

Subject

Complements

DEDUCTIVE

Purpose

Time:

Introduction **Body** **Conclusion**

I.

II.

III.

1.

A.

A.

A.

1.

B.

B.

B.

2.

2.

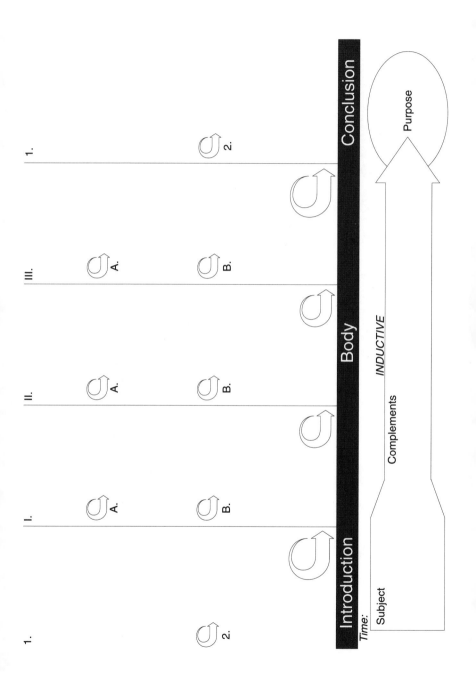

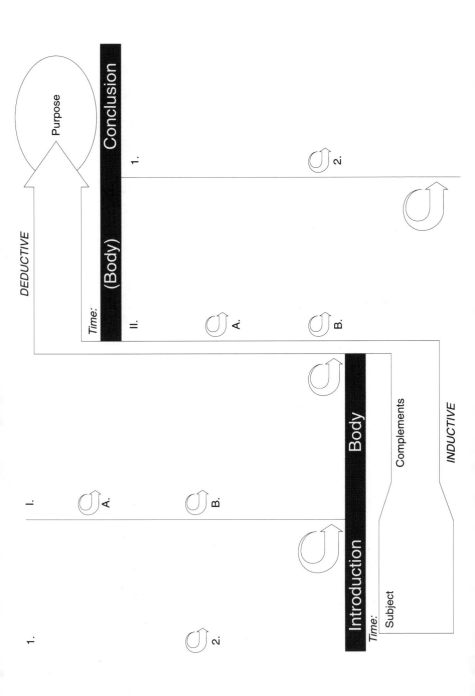

Bibliography

Adams, Jay E. *Preaching With Purpose: A Comprehensive Textbook on Biblical Preaching.* Grand Rapids: Baker, 1983.

Bailey, Raymond. *Jesus the Preacher.* Nashville: Broadman, 1990.

————. *Paul the Preacher.* Nashville: Broadman, 1991.

Davis, Henry Grady. *Design For Preaching.* Philadelphia: Fortress, 1958.

Dutton, John L. *How to be an Outstanding Speaker.* Downers Grove, Ill: Heritage Arts, 1989.

Edwards, Betty. *Drawing on the Artist within: An Inspirational and Practical Guide to Increasing Your Creative Powers.* New York: Simon and Schuster, 1987.

————. *Drawing on the Right Side of the Brain.* New York: St. Martin, 1988.

Field, Syd, ed. *Screenplay: The Foundations of Screenwriting,* rev ed. New York: Dell, 1984.

————. *The Screenwriter's Workbook.* New York: Dell, 1988.

Frank, Milo O. *How to Get Your Point Across in Thirty Seconds or Less.* New York: Pocket Books, 1986.

Gibble, Kenneth L. *The Preacher as Jacob: A Paradigm for Pulpit Ministry.* San Francisco: Harper Religious, 1985.

Humes, James C. *The Sir Winston Method.* New York: William Morrow, 1991.

Kilpatrick, James J. *The Writer's Art*. New York: Andrews, McMeel and Parker, 1984.

Larsen, David L. *The Anatomy of Preaching*. Grand Rapids: Baker, 1989.

Lewis, Ralph L., with Gregg Lewis. *Inductive Preaching: Helping People Listen*. Wheaton, Ill.: Crossway, 1983.

Litfin, Duane. *Public Speaking: A Handbook for Christians*, 2d ed. Grand Rapids: Baker, 1992.

Lowry, Eugene L. *The Homiletical Plot*. Atlanta: John Knox, 1980.

Massey, James Earl. *Designing the Sermon: Order and Movement in Preaching*. Nashville: Abingdon, 1980.

Mawhinney, Bruce. *Preaching with Freshness*. Eugene, Ore.: Harvest House, 1991.

Robinson, Haddon W. *Biblical Preaching*. Grand Rapids: Baker, 1980.

Ryken, Leland. *How to Read the Bible as Literature*. Grand Rapids: Zondervan, 1984.

————. *The Literature of the Bible*. Grand Rapids: Zondervan, 1974.

Welty, Eudora. *One Writer's Beginnings*. Cambridge, Mass.: Harvard University Press, 1984.

Whitesell, Faris D., and Lloyd M. Perry. *Variety in Your Preaching*. Westwood, N.J.: Revell, 1954.

Wiersbe, Warren W., and David Wiersbe. *The Elements of Preaching*. Wheaton, Ill.: Tyndale, 1986.